LEARNING

TO

WORK

Edited by

Blanche Geer

 SAGE PUBLICATIONS *Beverly Hills / London*

Publisher's Note

The material in this publication originally appeared as a special issue of AMERI-CAN BEHAVIORAL SCIENTIST (Volume 16, Number 1, September/October 1972). The Publisher would like to acknowledge the assistance of the special issue editor, Blanche Geer of Northeastern University, in making this edition possible.

For information address:

SAGE PUBLICATIONS, INC.
275 South Beverly Drive
Beverly Hills, California 90212

SAGE PUBLICATIONS LTD
St George's House / 44 Hatton Garden
London EC1N 8ER

Printed in the United States of America

International Standard Book Number 0-8039-0320-0

Library of Congress Catalog Card No. 73-87855

FIRST PRINTING (this edition)

LEARNING TO WORK

CONTENTS

Editorial Foreword

The Story of the Project

Research is not an isolated phenomenon. In sociology, projects blend sanctioned concepts and methods with blind assumptions and routinized ways of organizing the work transmitted from one research generation to the next without much questioning. Personal and practical considerations intrude at crucial points. Decisions on what to study, where, and for how long become contingent on careers. The political temper of the country makes one topic, theory, or method more attractive than another. Committee meetings, poor health, students requiring help or about to strike—a host of legitimate demands—shrink the researcher's energies. Yet we report our research, for the most part, as if none of this was so.

Until sociology achieves the well-developed paradigm that Kuhn (1964) says it presently lacks, I believe the more we know about our work the better. One way to do this is to tell something of the times in which a particular project originated, its organization, and the technical, conceptual, and human problems met along the way. With this thought, I introduce these papers with a short history of the project of which they were a part.

In 1962, after six years of research in the Midwest on two projects directed by Everett Hughes (studying four years in a medical school; Becker et al., 1961; and two on a college campus; Becker et al., 1968), Howard S. Becker and I wanted to teach without abandoning research. Since openings in sociology departments were then scarce, and two sociologists similar in research interests unlikely to find positions in one place, we thought a third research project should be as flexible in design as possible.

At the medical school and the college, two or three observers were in the field full time for two years. This yields such a quantity of complex data that analysis and reporting takes two more years and benefits greatly from the kind of continuous collaboration possible only when researchers live in the same place. A series of short studies might solve the problem.

In our style of work, one observer in the field two or three months can complete his analysis and report within a year. Less complex and conceptually demanding, such studies might be discussed by mail and published as separate papers rather than in a monograph. (To be working on a second book, as we then were, cools enthusiasm for a third.) Realistically, if we were teaching, a long, holistic study (Weiss, 1968) would be impossible. Yet the fieldworker who reports such a study in separate papers feels uneasy. Experienced in the round, field studies ask for holistic analysis and book-length reporting. The most important relationships can fall between one separate paper and another.

Deciding to ask for five years of funding, we recognized that part-time research in a university would produce only four or five short studies—not enough to say much. I decided to have two assistants with me on my part of the project; Becker, one. Five people working five years could produce a dozen studies.

In expanding our numbers, we did not plan to divide the work so that assistants would become the hired hands described by Roth (1966). Having benefited so much from it on the medical school study with Hughes and Becker, I thought each fieldworker should carry his study through analysis to a final report. We would hire experienced observers, they would read each other's field notes and together develop a conceptual framework to be used in subsequent studies.

It may seem odd to have said so much about planning without coming to what was to be studied. Both Becker and I were interested in occupations and education. Occupational training was then in the news, as the Kennedy administration sought ways to retrain workers displaced by automation. The topic seemed good. We could build conceptually and substantively on the work of Hughes and his students in the sociology of work (Hughes, 1971: 417-427), and on our own recent studies in education. We were both fieldworkers; methodology was not in question.

A glance at the literature on occupational training showed little research on (1) apprentices, (2) private trade schools, (3) training courses in the armed services, or (4) on-the-job training (Becker, 1965). We eliminated vocational education in high schools, public technical schools, junior colleges, and professional schools. Since these programs usually last two or more years, they are too long to grasp in short studies.

Knowing we would have time for only ten or twelve studies, the fact that they fell into four categories meant doing only one or two in each. Comparing one type with another could not be a major goal, for we wanted to extend or narrow the boundaries of education in order to understand it better.

There had been much research on the school; it was becoming the sole model of education. This project would push to extremes and explore as many other models as we could find. This way of thinking was first familiar to me in the medical school study, when we sought to answer broad questions from Hughes' (1971: 302) work about level of effort (Becker et al., 1961). Did highly motivated medical students restrict their effort as industrial workers often do? We found they did not, but directed their efforts in ways faculty disliked. The finding set a conceptual boundary: some subordinated people do not restrict production. Later, we had found grades and examinations central to the understanding of a college campus (Becker et al., 1968). Would some form of testing be central to occupational training? A series of studies might answer such questions more rapidly than any other approach.

Entitled "Educational Experiences of Non-College Youth," the proposal was funded by the National Institute of Mental Health for June 1964 through May 1969. I would direct two research assistants at the Youth Development Center at Syracuse University (MH09205); Becker, one at the Institute for the Study of Human Problems at Stanford University (MH09222). In 1965, Becker moved his project to Northwestern University. I went to Northeastern University in 1968. Table 1 summarizes the work at each university.

Fourteen research assistants worked on the project—some only a few months; others, a year or more. They collected data in San Francisco, upstate New York, Chicago, Boston, and Turkey. There were both rural and urban trainees, most under 25 and without college education. Five studies focused on men, four on women. Table 2 summarizes the type of training studied and what sort of organization owned or controlled it.

In what follows, I provide more detail on studies not reported here, particularly on those done in the first year, which set the patterns of work used throughout the project.

When funds arrived, Becker hired a graduate student in anthropology, Clyde Woods, as research assistant. On a twelve-month year at the Youth

TABLE 1
CHRONOLOGY OF THE PROJECT

Year	Place	Researcher	Topic	Report
1964	Syracuse	Bucci	Law of occupational training	Working paper
	Stanford	Woods	Barber college	See this issue and "Learning the Ropes"[a]
	Syracuse	ViVona	Trade school survey	Working paper
	Syracuse	ViVona	Business school	"Learning the Ropes"[a]
	Syracuse	Haas	Guidance	Memoranda
1965	Syracuse	Haas	Nurses aides	"Learning the Ropes"[a]
	Syracuse	Haas	Union officials	See dissertation (Haas, 1970)
	Syracuse	Haas	Ironworker apprentices	This issue and (Haas, 1970)
1965	Northwestern	Marshall	Meat cutters' apprentices	This issue and dissertation (Marshall, 1970)
	Syracuse	Notkin	Beauty school	This issue
1966	Northwestern	Mennerick	Jail school	This issue and dissertation, (Mennerick, 1971)
1967	Syracuse	Bogdan	Door-to-door salesmen	This issue
	Syracuse	Young	Electronics plant	This issue
1968	Northwestern	Weiner	Religious organization	– –
	Northeastern	Sanow	Airline stewardesses	M.A. thesis (Sanow, 1969)
1968	Northeastern	Weissman	Comparison of four studies	Working paper
1969	Syracuse	Rosenblum	Job orientation program	– –
	Northeastern	Conrad	Background materials	– –
	Northeastern	Sanow	Introduction	Working paper
	Two conferences at Northeastern to plan these papers			
	Northwestern	Becker	Comparison of school and apprenticeship	This issue
1970-1972	Northeastern	Geer	Editing	This issue

a. Geer, B., J. Haas, S. J. Miller, C. ViVona, C. Woods and H. S. Becker (1968) pp. 209-233 in I. Deutscher and E. J. Thompson (eds.) Among the People. New York: Basic Books.

TABLE 2
TYPES OF OCCUPATIONAL TRAINING STUDIED

Educational type	Ownership or control	Occupation
Trade school	Local proprietor	Comptometer operators
Trade school	Small chain	Beauty operators
Trade school	National chain	Barbers
Course or program	National company	Vacuum cleaner salesmen
Course or program	National company	Encyclopedia salesmen
Course or program	Local company	Airline stewardesses
Course or program	Worldwide religious organization	Member-workers
Course or program	County jail	Students
Apprenticeship	Union local	Ironworkers
Apprenticeship	Employing stores	Meat cutters
On-the-job training	Industry	Factory workers
On-the-job training	Hospital	Nurses aides
Job orientation	Federal government	Factory workers

Development Center, I hired a law student, Rosemary Bucci, to look into state and federal law on occupational training. There were no experienced fieldworkers in the area and our budgeted salaries did not attract one. In the fall, I hired Jack Haas, who took my fieldwork course, and Charles ViVona, who visited all local trade schools interviewing staff and students. He would choose one school to study from these data.

In a working paper, ViVona reported on sixteen local trade schools. Several were like junior colleges, training secretaries and accountants, with two-year programs, staffs of twenty, extracurricular activities, and dormitories. Five smaller schools trained beauty operators. Their students lived on their own, attended for a year, and needed only an eighth-grade education to enroll. Still other schools offered courses in electronics, modeling, truck driving, and charm. Occasionally ViVona got no interview; the owner had decamped, leaving no forwarding address.

ViVona's work interested Haas in the articulation of high school, occupational training and work; Haas turned to the voluminous literature on high school guidance counsellors. Since their interest was in psychological testing rather than occupations, they seemed to have little information of the detailed sort we wanted.

In September, field notes began to arrive from Woods' study of a barber college on skid row in San Francisco. For 75 students, there were three teachers and no classes; students began at any time and almost at once started to cut hair in the school barber shop. With so few teachers, students turned to each other for instruction. Thinking of the medical school study, we expected students sharing such pressing problems to have a highly developed student culture (Becker et al., 1961). But was student culture possible when students did not move through school as a cohort (Becker, 1964) doing the same things at the same time?

Unable to tell much from Woods' still incomplete data, ViVona decided to study a prosperous trade school on the main street of Syracuse offering a three-month course in business machine operation. Together in one classroom, students were drilled and tested by the teacher until expert enough to get a job. Slow learners could stay on without paying more tuition until they reached standard speeds.

The owner-entrepreneur was an ethical and practical man, who felt he should guarantee students jobs to attract them. This meant satisfying employers. When business was good for firms employing his graduates, he planned branches of his school in other cities. When business was bad, he thought of abandoning the school and doing something else. We decided reputable owners of trade schools are economically sensitive. They gain no advantage by flooding the job market or promising students that graduation means a job.

Licensed trades presented another picture. Woods' barber college took no responsibility for placing graduates, many of whom union officials who examined them failed. If students passed, the state licensed them as apprentice barbers to seek work where they could.

For my class, Haas studied on-the-job training of nurses' assistants in a hospital. He found the well-taught class they attended frequently useless, since aides at work faced difficult tasks not yet covered in class. The simplest things came first in class; students felt little pressure. On nursing floors, demands from patients, nurses, and other workers were often in conflict, and there was great pressure to act rapidly. Since trainees were not hired unless needed on nursing floors, the program articulated training with work, but at a cost. When teacher, nurses, and fellow trainees were unavailable, patients taught the aide his job.

While Woods was still in the field, I spoke before public school educators who were amazed at the fifteen percent dropout rate at the barber college. The question remained before us as the project went on, for dropouts and rebellion were rare even in the most poorly run training schools we studied.

As Becker prepared to move from Stanford to Northwestern, we spent the summer at Syracuse drawing together the first year's work in a paper. I hoped to solve problems anticipated in the final reporting of the project, an experiment in multiple authorship by mail. ViVona, Haas, and Woods each drafted a section, while I edited. Stephen J. Miller (1970), then doing fieldwork on Harvard interns contributed the final section.

The difficult compilation and writing task helped us develop a shared vocabulary that made later thinking easier (Geer et al., 1968). The paper dealt with trainees' initial learning: where things and people are, the niceties of rank and privilege, who expects them to do what, at what time, and for how long. In each study reported, such learning came from a different source: fellow students, the teacher, patients, and for Miller's interns, both medical students and residents. Calling this situational learning, we thought trainees who failed to learn were in a poor position to absorb their trade's technical parts.

With appointments in both the sociology department and the Youth Development Center, I was finding that teaching, committees, and graduate students had a way of taking priority, although 80% of my time was project-sponsored. Five of ten research assistants were also graduate students working with me on theses or dissertations, largely as a consequence of the eleven-month year at Y.D.C. In an entirely academic setting, Becker had three of his four research assistants as graduate students, too, and took summers off but neither of us had time to do the fieldwork we had planned.

Working with project members meant not only commenting on their field notes, but also introducing them to symbolic interaction as a conceptual framework for observing and analyzing data. Following Mead (1934), Hughes (1971: 348-354), Blumer (1969), and Becker (1970), observers tried to see the training situation through trainees' eyes (Geer, 1970). Each developed working hypotheses in the field (Geer, 1964: 331-337) and built tentative models of the situation as the participating groups perceived it (Becker et al., 1961: 33-48). As some assistants gained confidence, Becker and I sent memoranda suggesting ways of verifying field hypotheses (Bruyn, 1966) and things to read for sensitizing concepts. We drew attention to constant themes, noted variations, compared studies with each other, and discussed what dimensions of training should be studied next.

Although everyone on the project used the literature on occupations and education, each observer combed the library for material in his own larger area. For example, Haas read widely on lower-class culture; Notkin, Young, and Sanow, on women; Bogdan, on salesmanship; and Mennerick, on jails and prisons. Finding her data required more concepts about individuals than our emphasis on group perspectives supplied, Young read phenomenology.

Even the shorter studies were holistic (Weiss, 1968) in the sense that fieldworkers began with broad rather than limiting hypotheses and sought to grasp as much of the trainees' situation as they could. While participant observation was the chief method of collecting data, Woods used a questionnaire and Notkin systematically interviewed beauty students at work after they graduated from school. Documents, ranging from cartoons on bulletin boards to textbooks and union regulations, went into field notes.

Negotiating with the people in charge for access to everything and explaining themselves openly to all as sociologists, fieldworkers made their own research bargains (Geer, 1970: 82-86). Succeeding in fourteen of eighteen tries, they established a neutral role not identified with any faction that permitted talk with anyone in the training setting or people in control outside it (Geer, 1964: 325-327). Haas, for example, interviewed union and management officials in charge of the apprenticeship program and attended their joint meetings; Mennerick, talked with officials of the jail in which his school was located.

As necessary, observers also followed students outside the immediate training situation. Bogdan knocked on doors with trainees trying to sell their first vacuum cleaner. Haas drank beer with ironworkers and apprentices in city bars. During meals and breaks, all fieldworkers participated casually while continuing to observe and get people talking about what their training meant.

Efforts to see the situation through trainees' eyes sometimes led to difficult experiences. Marshall shivered for hours in refrigerated rooms watching men cut meat. Taking out life insurance, Haas climbed ladders to reach apprentices working twenty stories above the ground. Young shared the noise and confusion of a factory with women workers.

For several months—in some cases almost a year (Haas, Marshall, Notkin, and Mennerick)—observers spent up to six hours a day in the field and returned home to dictate field notes as soon as possible. Gradually, they learned to report conversations at length, in words and syntax close to the speaker's own. They described the gestures that add meaning to words and became sensitive to posture, pace of movement, facial expression, and clothing as still other modes of communication.

Fieldwork completed or nearly so, each observer turned to analysis of data. The longer studies were briefed on key-sort cards and coded in simple, nonconceptual categories (students, classes, tools, and the like) to facilitate retrieval of data. (To code with unrefined concepts permits many items to escape the retrieval process and prevents testing of tentative models.) With a few additions, categories developed for Haas' ironworkers served for other studies. Coding overlapped: everything conceivably related to a·category went into it, permitting the analyst to reassess the fit of concepts developed in the field and relate them to each other in a final model. (Later Weissman used the key-sort cards to pull out data· on trainees' presentation of self in four of the studies.)

Using the same method of collection and analysis of data and sharing a conceptual framework increased communication on the project and the amount of help we could give each other. It did not mean that other sociological approaches were entirely omitted. How one collects data inevitably limits the kind of conclusions that can be reached. Surveys, for example, usually restrict the researcher to conclusions about the opinions of people who do not interact; experiments, to laboratory situations; participant observation, to individuals and groups in interaction. As a result, the survey analyst speculates about action; the experimenter, about natural events; the participant observer, about the influence of groups beyond the boundaries of his study. Although we used questionnaires and formal interviews with scattered people as appropriate, we knew most about the groups that came together in the training situations studied. Our surest conclusions must rest on these data.

Other conceptual frameworks enter when the researcher tests his model by searching for alternative models that fit the data equally well—a process that may begin in the field but is most intense during data analysis. Haas, for example, asked himself whether the rough kidding apprentice ironworkers got from journeymen arose situationally in the training setting or was merely evidence of journeymen's working-class culture. He concluded that while working-class in style, the kidding carried so much technical information useful to apprentices that a situational explanation took more data into account.

The last year of the project saw two conferences held in Boston to discuss drafts of these papers and to plan others. I will now let the papers speak for themselves, but note in conclusion some educational dimensions of occupational training that cut across several studies. Each appears in differing emphasis; sometimes as the chief focus of a paper, at other times, implicit.

Along a first dimension—control of training—we see two extremes. Marshall's chief emphasis is the effect of company control; Haas' analysis of journeyman-apprentice interaction clearly shows union control. Mennerick's focus is control of students by groups outside the school; Notkin's paper describes a highly independent school, well-run by its staff.

A second dimension—the substantive fit of training and work—appears in four papers. Bogdan presents an extreme example; teachers use techniques on students which students learn to use on clients. Notkin's school achieves a good fit by less-unconventional methods. At the other end of the dimension, Young shows how certain teaching omissions may benefit students on the job; Mennerick shows teachers struggling on when they feel their training can have little effect.

A third dimension—the articulation of training with employment—appears in my discussions of ViVona's business school, Haas' nurses aides, and Woods' barber students in the introduction. While on-the-job training solves the problem of oversupply for nurses' aides, ViVona's is a trade school sensitive to the job market; Woods' school leaves the matter in the hands of outside examiners.

Three studies touch briefly on a fourth dimension—the fit of classes to on-the-job training. Marshall describes a poor fit; Haas' nurses aides (introduction), another; Bogdan implies a good fit.

Testing and evaluation make a fifth dimension mentioned in six papers. A dominant theme for Haas' ironworking apprentices, it is important for Young's factory workers to fill their quotas, Bogdan's salesmen to make a sale, Notkin's beauty students to get tips and returning patrons. Woods. barber students "psych out" union examiners; Mennerick's escape all testing.

The openness of the learning situation, whether students must learn on their own or can tap other sources, is a sixth dimension prominent in three papers, a chief emphasis for Woods and Notkin, while Marshall presents a negative case.

A seventh dimension—opportunity for self-evaluation—ties closely to open learning and testing. Four papers touch on it: Woods, Haas, Notkin, and Young.

Cohort processing of students—an eighth dimension—may be isolated from testing and self-evaluation. In some respects, it is the other extreme of open learning, appearing prominently in Bogdan. Its absence may be assessed in Woods, Haas, Marshall, and Mennerick. Notkin's school combines both cohort and open learning in constructive ways.

A ninth dimension—the sources of teaching authority—central to Woods' thesis, figures by implication in Notkin, Haas, and Bogdan. (The list is not exhaustive; I am sure the reader can distinguish still other dimensions.)

A Final Word

Dimensional analysis of this type is not conclusive; it sensitizes the researcher to concepts requiring still more research. Can such dimensions be applied to education in ordinary schools? Becker has a partial answer in the final paper of this issue which draws on the project and literature on the school to construct alternative models of education.

One may also ask whether we found constants. Did anything cut across all the studies? Broadly speaking, the trainees studied wanted to and did learn their trades, even under the adverse conditions described by Woods. There were few dropouts; Marshall and Notkin observed complaining, but even this mild form of rebellion was rare.

How do we account for this? Is the working and middle-class population we studied especially motivated to learn? Field studies of training situations cannot answer this question. Insofar as we deliberately looked for extreme situations to study, although they do not represent a definable universe, I find it plausible that the training itself, varied as it was, suggests the answer.

To the methodological question with which we began: can anything be learned from a series of studies done by different people in different places and different situations? I can only answer for myself: Yes, for the project has been an arduous but informative undertaking.

—Blanche Geer
Northeastern University

REFERENCES

BECKER, H. S. (1970) Sociological Work. Chicago: Aldine.
——— (1965) "Non college youth," pp. 46-64 in R. W. Conant (ed.) The Public Library and the City. Cambridge, Mass.: MIT Press.
——— (1964) "Personal change in adult life." Sociometry 27 (March): 40-53.
——— B. GEER, and E. C. HUGHES (1968) Making the Grade: The Academic Side of College Life. New York: John Wiley.
——— and A. L. STRAUSS (1961) Boys in White: Student Culture in Medical School. Chicago: Univ. of Chicago Press.
BLUMER, H. (1969) Symbolic Interactionism. Englewood Cliffs, N.J.: Prentice-Hall.
BRUYN, S. (1966) The Human Perspective in Sociology. Englewood Cliffs, N.J.: Prentice-Hall.

GEER, B. (1970) "Studying a college," pp. 81-98 in R. W. Habenstein (ed.) Pathways to Data. Chicago: Aldine.

––– (1964) "First days in the field," pp. 322-344 in P. E. Hammond (ed.) Sociologists at Work. New York: Basic Books.

––– J. HAAS, S. J. MILLER, C. ViVONA, C. WOODS, and H. S. BECKER (1968) "Learning the ropes: situational learning in four occupational training programs," pp. 209-233 in I. Deutscher and E. J. Thompson (eds.) Among the People. New York: Basic Books.

HAAS, J. (1970) "From punk to scale: a study of high-steel ironworkers." Ph.D. dissertation. Syracuse University.

HUGHES, E. C. (1971) The Sociological Eye. Chicago: Aldine.

KUHN, T. (1964) The Structure of Scientific Revolutions. Chicago: Univ. of Chicago Press.

MARSHALL, H. (1970) "The educational experiences of meat cutting apprentices." Ph.D. dissertation. Northwestern University.

MEAD, G. H. (1934) Mind, Self and Society. Chicago: Univ. of Chicago Press.

MENNERICK, L. A. (1971) "The impact of the external environment on a county jail school." Ph.D. dissertation. Northwestern University.

MILLER, S. J. (1970) Prescription for Excellence. Chicago: Aldine.

ROTH, J. A. (1966) "Hired hand research." Amer. Sociologist 1 (August): 190-196.

SANOW, M. (1969) "Airline stewardesses: a variation on a life style." M.A. thesis. Northeastern University.

WEISS, R. S. (1968) "Issues in holistic research," pp. 342-350 in H. S. Becker et al. (eds.) Institutions and the Person. Chicago: Aldine.

Students Without Teachers

Student Culture at a Barber College

CLYDE M. WOODS
Department of Anthropology
University of California (Los Angeles)

We usually expect teachers to pass on to their students a prescribed body of knowledge by formal methods of instruction. I studied a barber college in which teachers did little teaching, and students developed methods of self-instruction probably less obvious in schools with more conscientious teachers. I gathered my data by participant observation in the school over a period of five months and by interviews with staff members and about 75% of the students.

Pacific Barber College (a pseudonym) is both school and barbershop. Located in the skid row section of a large western city, its clients are derelicts, winos, pensioners, and others taking advantage of low prices. The heterogeneous student body includes 75 men and several Negro women who range in age from 17 to 55, and come from lower-class backgrounds. Whites predominate (57%), but Black, Mexican, Filipino, and Oriental Americans are also represented. Over 50% did not complete high school. About half are married. There are recent high school graduates, retired men, and people being retrained on government funds; a large number previously held one or more unskilled or semi-skilled jobs. Students see barbering as steady, clean, well-paying work easily and inexpensively learned. For older men, barbering is a good way to supplement retirement funds. Several men plan to work their way through college; some younger students have nothing better to do.

THE LACK OF INSTRUCTION

Pacific is operated by three licensed barber-instructors. One manages the school for the absentee owner. In addition to a daily lecture and some floor instruction, he handles local business and administrative functions. A retired school teacher and ex-barber gives a daily lecture and supervises instruction on the floor, helped by the third instructor.

The course can be completed in six months and must be completed within one year. There are overlapping shifts daily. One-third of the students hold jobs and attend part-time. The course includes 100 hours of classroom instruction, and 1,025 hours of practical application and study time. At the end of the training, students are examined by the State Board of Barber Examiners to become licensed apprentice barbers. After eighteen months of practice in a regular barber shop, the apprentice is again examined by the board to become a journeyman barber. Only then can he own and operate his own shop.

The novice must acquire the rudiments of shaving and hair-cutting and overcome his fear of using untried skills on a human being. Most students are shocked, confused, and dissatisfied to find they receive little, if any, help (Geer et al., 1968: 214-218). The manager assigns chapters in the textbook and has students practice shaving on a wooden dummy.

> I guess we're supposed to be pretty much on our own, just go around and watch and study and practice. . . . I guess they just give you your tools when they figure you're ready and then you go ahead, but you don't know much about it.

On the second or third day, students get their tools and take chairs in the beginners' shop. The newcomer dons a white smock, puts a student license on the mirror behind his chair, and begins to barber. He performs his first service—a shave, haircut, or both—without an instructor's help. If available (a rare thing), an instructor can be called. Occasionally, an advanced student offers pointers. Some students get into trouble:

> Well, I was a little nervous about everything . . . the first time I shaved a guy I cut him from here to here [he puts one finger at the ear lobe and the other almost to the point of the chin] and that was on the first stroke of the razor! After that I wouldn't even pick up a razor for three months.

New students realize on their own that the instruction they expected is not forthcoming. A student of two days, asked if he had heard about the lack of instruction from other students, said, "No, nobody said anything to me. It's just what I've observed while I've been here." Students' solution to the problem includes self-help, trial and error, observation, and help from other students.

Students repeatedly told me that helping each other was the major source of learning at the barber college. A school rule forbidding this is seldom enforced. Management says the rule prevents the transmission of bad habits but does not provide sufficient formal instruction to make it unnecessary. The manager spends most of his day in an office from which he cannot see the three practicing rooms. The other two instructors have other duties—classroom lecturing, grading papers, dealing with customers, and student discipline. State law requires the presence of one instructor for each twenty students and one for each room. Since Pacific has three practicing rooms operating twelve hours each day and only two instructors, working eight-hour shifts, adequate instruction is impossible. Asked about his duties, an instructor replied, "I give a class and I'm responsible for all the testing . . . and I have to make change, be on the floor, and help students when they need it. There's more to this job than it looks like."

On my first day at the school, an "old-timer" of three months told me, "The students don't get hardly any instruction around here. The instructor just stands back and watches. . . . . Most of what we learn we have to get on our own." Realization that instructors do not help them increases anxiety about initial contacts with customers, yet most students continue the program. The dropout rate is less than fifteen percent.

STUDENT SOLUTIONS

Many find a solution in the character of the customers themselves. Most patrons of the beginners' room are the "down and outs" of urban society. Students call them bums, derelicts, alcoholics, winos, tramps, and creeps. New students find their customers a shock:

> I had this guy one day and I was shaving him and he fell asleep. And when he woke up he looked like he was sick or something . . . he said he was okay, he said . . . but when he got out of the chair he shit all over the floor. . . . I had to go outside and get some fresh air. It really stunk up the place.

New students see men only a few days more advanced than themselves shaving and cutting hair without serious consequences and think they can do the same:

> What the hell, they're only paying 25 cents for a haircut when they come in here. If they want a good haircut they can go uptown and get one for $2.25. You can't expect too much when you come in here. You pay 25 cents and you get a 25 cent haircut.

While this attitude may help a student through the first days of school, he soon finds that barbering is difficult and requires practice; using underdeveloped skills on a real person continues to be an anxiety-laden experience. In self-defense, he turns to fellow students for instruction.

Sometime between his third and fifth week, the novice moves to one of two advanced shops. He may choose either, but finds

Black students and customers use one room and non-Blacks the other. Movement to the advanced shops depends on the time spent in the beginners' shop, number of shaves completed, the student's desire to move, staff evaluation, and the availability of chairs. The move exposes the student to a different type of customer and a larger social network.

Where customers in the beginners' shop were primarily "down and outers," those in the advanced shops include pensioners, young children, students' friends, and people who want to take advantage of the $.75 price. These people are concerned about the quality of the service and demand respectful treatment:

> The main difference up here is that a customer will come in and sit down and tell you he wants so much off here and he wants his hair cut a certain way where in the back [room] they don't give a damn.

Here, novices meet students at many different stages of ability. Some have worked from 3 to 27 weeks; others are returning for the refresher course required of failees who want to repeat the examination. These, and a few with barbering experience in the military or the merchant marine, are important teaching resources.

Teachers teach even less in the advanced shops than they do in the beginners' shop. Students learn by observing student barbers considered superior in ability. A student told me, "I think that's the only way to learn—by watching somebody else and then practicing."

Help from other students is freely requested and openly offered:

> While John was tapering the hair with shears and comb in the back, one of the other students came up and said, "It's better to use the clippers on the back of a kid that size because he doesn't sit still long enough to let you really use the shears." Another student came around to the other side of the chair and said something similar to John and pretty soon he did take out the clippers and comb and use them instead.

To fill their quota, advanced students pick up additional shaves in the beginners' shop where shaves are more often requested. While there, they offer advice and demonstrations to beginning students.

The student who engages in a wide range of interaction acquires more knowledge and practical ability than the "loner." Joking about a bad haircut given by an advanced student, a student remarked, "That's the guy they say you can't even carry on a conversation with. . . . There's not a chance he could pass the exams." Two students an instructor praised for working hard and not "horsing around" were pointed out by some as loners, a description verified by my observation. About one loner, an instructor said, "He doesn't sit around and talk . . . with the guys . . . but he works hard and I think he'll do all right." Several students commented that this student, in his fourth month, always started his taper too high. No one bothered to tell him about this. Asked why, a student says:

> I guess [instructors] don't see it or they don't care because they've never said anything about it. And he keeps making the same mistake. We could tell him, but then we would get in trouble.

This student cites the formal rule against student instruction—a rule few follow.

Evaluation and comparison also begins in the beginners' shop. A first-week student compares his performance to that of two other beginners:

> That Japanese fellow over there and that Filipino are both good barbers . . . but that one guy you know, he should be good, he's been cutting hair now for two years . . . you can't expect us to be as good as he is.

Judging oneself better than others is also common. A student of six weeks says, "Christ, there are guys up here who can't cut hair worth a damn. I've been watching them . . . for instance, that guy over there. I think I can do as well as most of these guys." There is considerable agreement, shared by instructors, on superior and inferior students. But the best indication of superior ability is often being watched performing a service and being asked for help by peers. When a service is completed and the customer walks toward the front of the shop to pay his bill, students at work, waiting for customers or just sitting around check him out. Bad haircuts receive the most attention:

> Boy, you just missed the best example of a bad haircut that ever walked out of here. . . . He had three lines around the back of his neck and it looked just like a bowl had been put over his head.

Students vary in their relative emphasis on quantity and quality: "You know, its important to do a good job too, besides going fast. You wait until you get up before the board. They don't care how fast you go. They want to see a good job."

A student who constantly bragged about the number of services he could complete in a short time came under constant criticism. Occasionally, evaluation takes a more direct form:

> Alex, talking to Jake, says, "Now take you, for instance. I wouldn't hire you in a shop or recommend you. I mean, no reflection on your personality, but hell, I'd never know if you were going to come to work, if you were going to be drunk, or what you'd do."

Shortage of instructors and inefficient use of their time means little instruction, and the rule against peer teaching is difficult to enforce. Further, staff encourage students to observe. Selection of chairs on a first-come-first-served basis shuffles students so that each has different neighbors daily. The overlap in shifts and part-time students who come in at their own convenience widen the range of interaction. Moving from chair to chair and room to room without restriction, students can easily seek out others for help or join in bull sessions.

PREPARATION FOR EXAMINATIONS

In addition to logging 1,250 hours at the school, advanced students must complete a stipulated number of specific services before taking the state examinations—550 haircuts, 150 shaves, 15 rolling cream massages, 25 rest facials, 15 facial treatments, 25 shampoos, 20 scalp treatments, and 10 tonics. To fulfill these requirements, the ideal student works hard, takes all comers, and does not horse around—an ideal more often expressed than practiced. "That's the only way you can get out of here, by just taking as many customers as you can get." Another remarks, "Man, I'll cut anybody's hair. Anybody who comes in and sits down in my chair. . . . I am here to learn and complete my services."

But there are problems. The occasional scarcity of chairs and (more common) scarcity of customers stems from the nature of the school and its clientele. Student competition for certain kinds of customers, cheating, and horsing around instead of working are problems rooted in students' personal character-istics and the social structure of the school.

The scarcity of chairs and customers varies with enrollment and customer traffic. During a period of increased enrollment, one student complained he had a chair for only two hours over a three-day period. It is worse in the beginners' shop, since students from the advanced shops return to pick up shaves. Staff members sometimes remove an absent student's tools and release the chair to someone else when the absentee tries to hold his chair by neglecting to "break down" during a lunch, lecture, or study break. Competition for chairs is most common during the middle of the day when shifts overlap. Students with chairs furthest away from the front are at a disadvantage since customers who get much beyond the door are often least desirable, so students try hard to get front chairs. For early shift, this means arriving earlier than the others. The afternoon shift must be on the spot when students break down. I observed some waiting as long as an hour for a desirable chair.

Competition for customers to work on is another feature of student interaction. Some jump out of their chairs and holler at customers when they enter; others walk to the door, put an apron on the client, and escort him to their chair. Some recruit from other rooms. Major variables are the customer's appearance (cleanliness, dress), amount and style of hair, ethnic background, and tipping possibilities. Students in different stages of training prefer different hairstyles to work on.

Students also differ in their disposition to work. There are "hard workers"; and "goof-offs." The hard worker does more work on a greater variety of customers and takes anyone who comes through the door when his chair is empty. He horses around less than the goof-off, who is choosy, lazy, and fools around rather than working. Most students fall between the two types; few take everyone. One way of ensuring against undesirable customers is to leave the chair when they come in. Instructors must often direct customers to particular students to ensure them of service.

Cheating is another way to fill time and service requirements. Some students fail to punch the time clock when off duty. The manager makes spot checks. When caught, violators receive a written reminder on their timecard.

Most students horse around at one time or another. Students working on a customer are exposed to good-natured raillery, "God, man, what have you done? Look at that line in back! This poor guy won't even be able to walk out on the street without being laughed at." When asked about the secret of success at Pacific, a student in his sixth month responded:

> A lot of guys get kidded . . . a lot of horsing around, and you've just got to be able to take it. Some of the guys are hotheaded . . . but they still take it and dish it out and they've got to be able to do this or they wouldn't be able to get along.

Horsing around is a form of social interaction which must be tolerated and mastered by those who want help in learning. Even students who dislike it succumb occasionally. After three students had complained at length to me about the horsing around, I observed them kidding a customer about tipping and paying his bill. When it was over, one of them said, "See, even Roy does it once in awhile. . . .I guess it's just the way this place is. Everybody acts funny a lot of the time." A student recently transferred from a more rigidly organized barber school said, "I don't think I've changed at all except that I've kind of fallen into the pattern around here. . . . I get choosy about customers. . . . I sort of mess around some days. . . . I just sit around and shoot the shit like everybody else." Most students engage in horsing around, although it interferes with study and work.

Students are required to learn a certain amount of academic material about the skin, the fundamentals of electricity, and the human nervous system. They read this material and have it read to them by instructors, but still fear they will fail the state board examination. Despite ineffective study methods, most students pass that portion of the examination; apparently constant catechism commits it to memory.

Students worry a great deal about passing other parts of the state board examination. Many think them a racket and the grading capricious. They design schemes to beat the system—paying off the examiners, having a master barber do most of the work on the model used in the examination, finding out the contents of the test before taking it.

I observed seventy candidates take state examinations for apprentice and journeyman licenses. Two examiners tested a large number of candidates simultaneously, so many that they could not observe any one closely. In the end, by their own testimony, the examiners grade largely on the look of the completed haircut and shave. Examiners estimate that sixty percent taking the test the first time pass; ninety percent, they say, pass on the second try; the rest, the third time. Of the twenty Pacific students taking the test (half on the second try), twelve passed. Since students vary so much in how seriously they work and prepare for examinations, it should be possible to predict who will pass. But the manager of the school said he could not predict; some good students fail.

Those who fail must either give up the idea of barbering or return to school for additional training. Most return, feeding semi-skilled personnel back into the system of peer instruction. These students are not criticized for their failure, even for the second time. Many students expect to fail once or twice, since a large percentage does. They see students fail whom they consider superior or equal in ability to themselves.

I've seen some of these guys that have gone up for their exams and I know how much better barbers they are than I am. . . . I mean, I know how good they are and they fail and it makes me wonder how I'll do.

Students think somebody has to fail; even experts have trouble predicting success. They return, understandably disappointed, but determined to try again and even a third time if necessary.

CONCLUSION

From the outset of their training, students confront the problem that their teachers do not teach. The anxiety they feel working on real customers dies as they adopt the belief that these people care little about what happens to them.

Advanced students learn by trial and error, observation, and assistance from peers when further experience confirms how little instruction from teachers there is. Learning to learn from peers is not a matter of forming cliques; rather, it means learning to evaluate the skills of other students in comparison to one's own and mixing freely with many, good barbers and bad. The loner, even the student who restricts his interaction to a few others, cannot take advantage of the accumulated knowledge of the rest of the student body. A loose network of social relations with whatever students are on hand makes learning from peers possible.

REFERENCE

GEER, B., J. HAAS, S. J. MILLER, C. ViVONA, C. WOODS, and H. S. BECKER (1968) "Learning the ropes," pp. 209-233 in I. Deutscher and E. J. Thompson (eds.) Among the People. New York: Basic Books.

Binging

Educational Control Among High Steel Ironworkers

JACK HAAS
Department of Sociology and Anthropology
McMaster University (Hamilton, Ontario)

Conventional thinking about education is usually limited to situations where teachers impart knowledge to students. The process is unilateral; information flows from superior to subordinate, and we look for and evaluate change only in students. We might better consider education an interactive process in which all participants are affected, and their relations are highly variable. The relationship of teacher to student is not limited to the superior-subordinate model. In some situations, peer or colleague relations develop; in other situations, students control teachers. Above all, we must recognize the developing character of these relations, characterized by flux and situational redefinition (Geer, 1968).

In the broadest sense, all interaction is educational, but in schools we deliberately attempt to change people. As mechanisms of social control, schools and training evaluate, punish, and reward. In this paper, I show how such mechanisms of control vary with the relations of participants in different settings. I describe a social device used in training ironworker apprentices—a device that serves a number of purposes related to social control. Ironworkers use it to test self-control and trustworthiness in others. They use it to establish temporary status in work settings where competence is unclear. Finally, they use it to communicate group expectations and job-related information difficult to share another way. Implicit in its use is its appropriateness for guiding others' actions. The device, which I call "binging" (Roethlisberger and Dickson, 1934), fulfills the same purposes as examinations and grades in ordinary schooling.

BACKGROUND

I spent nine months as a participant observer of ironworkers and their apprentices in the union hall and after work. I followed the construction of a 21-story building and visited other work sites. On the first day of fieldwork, two questions emerged. How could high steel ironworkers, on narrow steel beams high above the ground, go about their work with such nonchalance and confidence? And why were kidding and ridicule such a dominant part of their interaction?

In most educational settings, standard ways of exchanging information and evaluating this exchange have developed. Teachers lecture, students answer questions, teachers' grade answers. In apprentice situations, such exchange and evaluation is more subtle. The ironworker's situation, where the threat of injury or death is pervasive, poses problems in both the exchange of information and evaluation of coworkers.

A continuous problem is trust. Safety depends on the actions of coworkers. A mistake can mean death. Ironworkers use two kinds of tests to determine trustworthiness. One test involves watching fellow workers "run the iron." Verbal harassment of other workers tests their self-control.

For the neophyte ironworker, running the iron is a crucial test. The new apprentice must work high above ground with nothing beneath him but a four- to eight-inch beam. He receives no training or advice about maintaining his balance or maneuvering across the steel. He runs the iron before the critical eyes of other workers. His only clue to proper performance is the performance of other workers. The poise and confidence they display tell him what his colleagues expect.

Workers recognize that running the iron is a managed performance and may not reflect one's true feelings. Yet it is important for workers to know whether a confident front (Goffman, 1959) will break down in a crisis. Workers believe it is important to know as much as possible about the trustworthiness of fellow workers in all sorts of situations, and they test this by binging, a process similar to styles of interaction observed in black ghetto youth (Kochman, 1969), white lower-class gang members (Miller et al., 1961), hospital personnel (Goffman, 1951: 122), and perhaps as Eric Berne (1964) suggests, Americans in general. These studies indicate the many purposes of this form of interaction. Everett Hughes (1945: 356) points out an important use of binging in testing newcomers:

> To be sure that a new fellow will not misunderstand requires a sparring match of social gestures. The zealot who turns the sparring match into a real battle, who takes a friendly initiation too seriously, is not likely to be trusted with the lighter sort of comment on one's work or with doubts and misgivings; nor can he learn those parts of the working code which are communicated only by hint and gesture. . . . In order that men may communicate freely and confidently, they must be able to take a good deal of each other's sentiments for granted.

In the following quotation from my field notes, a journeyman, three apprentices, and the observer engage in a sparring match, on top of an emerging 21-story building.

> Abe, the journeyman says, "These fucking apprentices don't know their ass from a hole in the ground." The journeyman turns to me and says, "I hope you don't think these guys are representative of the whole apprenticeship. They're a pretty sad lot." Joining in with the kidding, I say, "Yeh, I've noticed that." Bud, an apprentice, says to me, "Don't listen to him. He's just a fucking Indian." The

journeyman responds, "Yeh, and he's a fucking nigger." Abe then yells down to an apprentice below, "What the fuck are you doing down there, playing with yourself? For Christ sakes get up here and bring that machine up here with you."

The example suggests how repartee tests relationships and exchanges information. The style is characteristically earthy. There is little regard for amenities, and the jibes seem deliberately provocative—a verbal challenge. In a dangerous work situation where we expect workers to try to ease conflict, we find deliberate provocation. An Indian journeyman sums up the importance of this form of interaction as he and I drink beer in a bar:

> You see, I don't get upset often. And when I do I forget right after. You've got to figure, if you're going to work with the guy, you can't hold something against him, because he could kill you and you could kill him. You forget fast when you're in this business. What you do is try to see what the guy's made of, because if he gets agitated, and wants to fight over something like this, then you don't know what he's going to do up on the steel if something goes wrong. A lot of times you're responsible for that other guy up there and you can either make him or break him.

USES OF BINGING

Workers use binging to test trustworthiness and self-control. Will a man keep cool under blistering personal attacks? If he loses his poise, it indicates he may lose control in other threatening situations—e.g., high above the ground. If he takes such kidding too seriously, he may carry a grudge into a situation where vengeance is easy.

Binging also conveys information about expected relationships among participants. They are relationships characterized by constant redefinition, indicated by subtle cues from participants. The interaction permits the apprentice to experiment by binging back in anticipation of a favorable response, which shows journeymen consider him acceptable.

By binging several apprentices, a journeyman shows himself

superior to all. That all apprentices are not equal becomes clear when one apprentice calls the journeyman a "fucking Indian," while another accepts the journeyman's strong words without reply.

The one-sided nature of binging between journeymen and apprentice was quite obvious throughout the study. New apprentices are called "punks," and their role involves carrying out the most demeaning tasks and accepting the deliberate castigation of veteran workers.

> On the top of the building, I talk with a journeyman about his constant kidding of new apprentices. I say, "Looks like you were busting Jerry, the firewatch, the other day?" Abe [journeyman] says, "That's all right, I used to have to take it even worse than that. You see, I started pretty young. I used to work summers at this, and they had me doing all sorts of punking, and everyone was on my ass, all the time. I remember one summer, I carried bolts around, and that's all. I got so fucking sick of looking at those bolts, I was about ready to go out of my nut. If I took it, these guys can take it. You've got to take it and dish it right back."

As this journeyman makes clear, binging is an institutionalized part of the apprentice career. It is an initiation all must pass through before acceptance as a peer who can "dish it right back."

The changing nature of workers' relations and the use of binging to mark changes cannot be overstressed. Ironworkers see their relations with each other as ambiguous. Workers change jobs frequently, and the labor force changes daily. Men vary in skill and experience. A man may be a leader in some phase of the work, an inexpert follower in others. Thus, workers continually face the problem of defining themselves vis-à-vis other workers. Binging provides them with a mechanism for creating a social order out of an ambiguous and unstructured environment. In the following example, an apprentice underlines the problem:

> As we walk off the job site I ask, "These guys give you the business about being an apprentice?" Jim, the apprentice, says, "No, not

these guys too much. I mean they kid you all the time. It's the older guys. They expect you to go and take their tools up in the morning and take their tools down at night, and go around kissing their ass. I set them straight right away and say, "Hey look, I'm not a laborer. I'm an apprentice. They'll kid you about being a punk."

As this apprentice indicates, the punk label may be difficult to overcome. Special efforts may be required to convince others it is no longer appropriate. By binging, an individual may "live up to" or "live down" the labels assigned.

The chief difference between apprenticeship and other kinds of training is that neophytes are thrust into the actual work environment. For some trades, immediate entry may not create problems, but ironworker apprentices' acts may have serious consequences. Other kinds of training may allow mistakes, but ironworkers cannot afford them, and an apprentice cannot look incompetent.

In such a situation, apprentices hesitate to ask questions, which of themselves, indicate incompetence. The obvious dilemma is how the unskilled can learn the job without revealing their ignorance.

They learn some skills by observing, but sometimes there are no opportunities to observe. Furthermore, journeymen lack ways of determining what an apprentice knows. Exchanging information by binging solves this problem as it permits all participants to teach, and the work group protects itself by passing information on in everyday interaction. Such exchanges are almost always subtle, but the information is there for those who need it.

In the following example, Abe, a journeyman, has been kidding Joe, an apprentice, about sexual matters. He charges that Joe associates with an undesirable prostitute and a homosexual. This one-sided attack was being relished by a small group of apprentices and journeymen when the foreman approached:

Mike, the foreman, comes over and says to Joe "Go over there on the new section, on the planks, and count the guy lines. Spread them out on the beams." Joe looks confused and shrugs his shoulders. Abe kids Joe, "Get the fuck over there and count the guy lines. You know what guy lines are?" Mike walks back. Abe says, "Mike, you know he's only been an ironworker for a couple of weeks." Mike says, "Yeh, guess he can count though. Can't he?" Everyone laughs. In the meantime Joe was on the planking picking up steel beams and moving them. He was obviously goofing badly. Abe walks over and yells, "Not that, you stupid fuck. Count the guy lines. Look, just spread them out across the beam where there's some support for them. They're too heavy just on the planking. And just count them and tell me how many you've got. Okay?" Abe stands there laughing while Joe nods his head in understanding.

The journeyman abuses the apprentice, then saves him from an embarrassing mistake and a potentially dangerous action—piling steel beams on wood planking. His help tells the apprentice that the kidding is not serious and indicates acceptance, not rejection. Moreover, the apprentice, without asking, has found someone to help him.

Information exchanged in binging may be intended for a larger audience. In this example, the work group has just finished lunch and stands at the bottom of the structure awaiting the back-to-work whistle. Two journeymen and three apprentices are together:

Al [journeyman] points to the emerging structure and says, "I was up there and he's [foreman] telling me to put this beam in place. And he's looking this way and he's pointing the other way. So Christ, I don't know where the hell to look." Irish [journeyman] says, "Yeh, he's always looking at you and you never know it." Al says, "Can you imagine Bill [apprentice] and him together? Bill's the same way. One eye going the wrong way. They'd both be looking at each other and neither seeing what the other's seeing." This really brings laughter. Al continues, "That bastard Bill, trying to get into my fifteen year old babysitter. He should have known that's my preserve."

This is a warning: Don't trust the gestures of certain workers. Although presented with levity, it is critically important. Noise and the physical separation of workers make gestures a key means of communication. Ironworkers have an elaborate set of hand signals for bringing steel beams into position, and it is important to be able to take these gestures for granted, to assume they are accurate. The journeyman has warned apprentices not to accept all gestures at face value.

CONCLUSION

Binging allows journeymen to teach without openly questioning an apprentice's competence. As a test of poise and courage, it adds to the information a man reveals about himself while running the iron. It provides a way to establish trust as well as a way to improve the trustworthiness of others by providing them with important information. At once aggressive and subtle, it is useful for checking on and realigning others' actions. It is an important mechanism of social control that also helps the apprentice to find himself in a complex and ambiguous social setting.

In schools and other educational settings more formal than the ironworker apprenticeship, books and lectures provide information, examinations test it, and grades establish the learner's status in relation to his fellows. But the binging of ironworkers goes farther. By laying the groundwork for trust between apprentice and journeyman, it opens the door to eventual equality between learner and teacher.

REFERENCES

BERNE, E. (1964) Games People Play. New York: Grove.

GEER, B. (1968) "Teaching," pp. 560-565 in Volume 15 of the International Encyclopedia of the Social Sciences. New York: Macmillan and Free Press.

GOFFMAN, E. (1959) Presentation of Self in Everyday Life. New York: Doubleday Anchor.

——— (1951) Encounters. Indianapolis, Ind.: Bobbs-Merrill.

HUGHES, E. C. (1945) "Dilemmas and contradictions of status." Amer. J. of Sociology 5 (March): 353-359.

KOCHMAN, T. (1969) " 'Rapping' in the black ghetto." Trans-action 6 (February): 26-34.

MILLER, W. B., H. GEERTZ, and H.S.G. CUTTER (1961) "Aggression in a boy's street-corner gang." Psychiatry 24 (November): 283-298.

ROETHLISBERGER, F. L. and W. J. DICKSON (1934) Management and the Worker. Boston: Harvard University Graduate School of Business Administration.

Structural Constraints on Learning

Butchers' Apprentices

HANNAH MEARA MARSHALL

Department of Sociology
Northern Illinois University

The meat cutting apprenticeship in a midwestern American metropolitan area can be a boring and frustrating experience.[1] On the job in the meat departments of supermarkets, apprentices rarely learn any but the most unskilled and peripheral tasks of the occupation. A few apprentices attend a trade school class and learn important tasks, yet spend much time on activities which seem to them useless. In this paper, I show how they learn what they do and why their desire to learn more is frustrated.

Everett C. Hughes (1951) suggested it would be useful to think of an occupation as a bundle of tasks. To practice an occupation, a person learns one, a few, or all tasks in the bundle. Apprentices want to learn the central tasks in the bundle called meat cutting and are unhappy when permitted to learn only some.

In large chain supermarkets, meat cutters often specialize, and apprentices say they have little opportunity to move from one task to another. They want to learn to do what journeymen do every day on the job. In every store, some journeymen cut and saw meat expertly. Respected by fellow workers, these men form the spiritual center of the workplace.

Apprentices complain that they work only at the wrapping machine. A States Wide[2] apprentice said, "I've been wrapping as long as I've been here—two months. Some apprentices do it almost two years." At Urban Center, an apprentice explained:

> I haven't learned anything down here. . . . I don't think there's much you can do [about it]. You can watch whenever you get a chance. I guess that's what you're supposed to do. Like if you're boating [putting meat in containers] in the cutting room you're supposed to watch while you're doing that . . . like you can watch the guy on the saw and see where he makes the cuts and how he does it. Then when you get an opportunity like during slack times you won't waste it. . . . When I first got here I used to eat my lunch in 15 minutes and spend 45 minutes watching the guy on the saw. . . . I really tried to learn as much as I could. But that didn't do me no good. . . . They still didn't give me any opportunity. So after a few weeks I just did my job and nothing more.

Some try less, but most apprentices experience frustration in learning more than the most peripheral tasks.

PROBLEMS IN LEARNING

Apprentices also experience learning problems in the trade school. They find the class dull because they learn few journeymen's tasks. Learning to cut meat with a knife and an automatic saw is important, but other things they do in class are irrelevant to present and future jobs.

Students try to put in time as effortlessly as possible. As one said, "It's boring. I'd like to get outta here." This was not a rare statement. Students were seldom interested in what went on in the classroom or the school shop. One asked another, "Why hurry [with your lessons]? You have to come anyway." He replied, "I wanta jus' sit around and read the newspapers the way Smith does." Similar behavior occurred in the shop. My field notes say: "Mick and another student were cutting meat very slowly and arguing about what cylinder engine is found in a particular model of Chevrolet."

On the job, learning experiences vary with certain structural dimensions of the work settings. One such dimension, organizational purpose, greatly affects apprentices. Learning is possible only if it does not detract from the organization's purpose.

The purpose of running a meat department, I realized, is to sell meat at a profit; the purpose of the trade school class, to give a certificate. In each situation, teaching apprentices what they wanted to know was secondary. Apprentices could learn what they wanted if it did not interfere with making a profit or following a certification program.

A supermarket meat department manager tries to achieve an advantageous difference between the total volume of sales for the department and the wholesale price of his meat order, plus his costs for personnel and facilities. To do this, the manager sees to it that his skilled journeymen can prepare a large volume of meat efficiently by specializing in short, repetitive tasks. He puts apprentices where they can work for him most efficiently. Diverting journeymen from work to training tasks increases the short-run cost of selling meat. Because journeymen and apprentices are so occupied with profit-making tasks, apprentices rarely learn many tasks in the bundle for meat cutting.

Besides the cost of a journeyman's time, training apprentices have a potential cost in the mistakes they might make. At the wrapping machine, they can only waste paper and time, but mistakes with meat are costly. An assistant manager at Urban Center explained:

We have to see where we think they'll work well. We should train them but we're a very busy store. Production counts very much. Now if we were in a neighborhood store we'd have much more time to train apprentices but we've got to really put this stuff out. . . . Now [that] new apprentice . . . we couldn't put him in the wrapping room. . . . To be good in the wrapping room you need somebody who is quick with his hands. You know the little guy in there? . . . Well, he's very quick. He's very good with his hands. We had him in here [cutting room] some but we mostly have him out there [wrapping room] because we have to get it [meat] out and he gets it out right away. We have too many apprentices down here. Upstairs they act as if we've got all journeymen. They just count the number of men we have. Now when there's a slack we can move them around but if you can depend on a man in a certain place then you keep him there when you're busy.

Managers in stores all over the metropolitan area had similar problems with training. Even neighborhood stores could not free personnel from work to train apprentices.

THE TRADE SCHOOL

Apprentices learn one job like running the automatic wrapping machine. Since this is the least skilled task, it makes sense to give it to the man paid least. When apprentices learn to perform such a task dependably, they contribute to the smooth operation of the department. Unless needed elsewhere, they work at this task all day.

The manager is not the only person whose interests would be threatened if apprentices learned more tasks. Journeymen have purposes at odds with those of apprentices. They are interested in putting in a day's work with as little effort as possible by establishing a smooth pace. Training apprentices would interrupt regular work and add new tasks.

The class was started by the meat cutters' union to grant a certificate. The certificate equaled six months of the apprenticeship and entitled the holder to receive journeyman's pay and status after two and one-half years on the job. Now, under the jurisdiction of midwestern city board of education, its purpose remains the same.

To justify awarding the certificate, the trade school class runs in traditional fashion, with book work and written examinations in class and practice in shop. The work follows the same pattern year after year without reference to apprentices' need to learn useful things not learned on the job. Teachers teach techniques in use when they worked in retail markets that are readily adaptable to a school setting. To be more responsive to students' interests would make more work for teachers.

The classroom curriculum is similar to courses on other subjects. Students read books and write assignments and examinations. When they have attended the school for a predetermined number of hours and completed all assignments and examinations, they earn a certificate. Most assignments are not relevant to the supermarket. For instance, students learn to make wholesale cuts not used in stores, or to advise customers in cooking meat. Because these are not skills in demand, few students bother to learn them. They look up answers in the book rather than reading the assignment, help each other with examinations, and snooze through movies. But they get that certificate.

Apprentices are more interested in the shop period, where they become familiar with equipment they hope to use someday at work. But the shop, too, has tasks useless in a supermarket. One of the first things learned is how to sharpen a knife—a vital task only in the past. Today, a company delivers sharpened knives to and collects dull ones from meat departments at regular intervals. Students practice making rolled roasts by hand-tying knots, while in supermarkets, now, journeymen use an automatic knot-tying machine for this task. Apprentices go through the motions of learning to earn the certificate, but soon become disenchanted with the school.

The physical layout of a work setting is an important dimension of learning, since apprentices get a great deal from observing others and being observed. Some meat departments were laid out so that apprentices working at the wrapping machine could not watch journeymen cut and saw meat. An apprentice's feeling about this separation came out when a district manager in a large, local market told him to return poorly arranged trays of meat to the journeymen.

> I'm scared to go in the back room. I feel so out of place there. I haven't gone back there in a long time because I just don't know what to do when I'm there. All those guys know so much about meat cutting and I don't know anything.

Apprentices feel isolated when they cannot hear what journey-men say or watch them as they cut meat.

It is interesting to contrast this apprentice's experience with that of an apprentice at States Wide Chain. He also worked only at the wrapping machine, but in the same room as the journeymen. He heard and saw everything they did and was familiar with how they went about their work.

The classroom and the shop of the trade school were laid out so that apprentices could observe everyone there. In the classroom, they worked on assignments sitting three to a table. The class was informal; students looked, sometimes even walked around to observe what was happening. It was hardly ever quiet. Students talked to each other; the teacher talked to individual students in a tone of voice which other students could hear. While working on individual assignments, students learned by hearing and participating in discussions with the teacher and fellow students. They often hear apprentices discuss with the teacher problems they had on the job.

During shop, they worked facing each other along a table, and each could observe the technique of several others. They listened to or participated in one or more conversations at a time. New students saw immediately how experienced ones worked.

The apprentices were in different stages of the course and came from different stores in different parts of the metro-politan area. In such close proximity, each could learn from those ahead of him. Each heard the experiences of apprentices in a number of stores. This helped him to evaluate his own situation and decide whether to try to get a better job in another store. Those in small, independent chains learned of benefits like profit-sharing offered by large chains, and some changed jobs.

At school and work, organizational purposes may fail to take account of an apprentice's desire to learn the bundle of tasks current in his occupation. The physical layout of a store or classroom, often related to purpose, can facilitate watching and talk between neophyte and expert. By making these difficult, it can seriously hamper an apprentice's efforts to learn.

Size is still another dimension of learning. Supermarket meat departments vary in the number of apprentices they hire, and this results in differences in the apprentices' learning experiences. In larger settings with more apprentices, they learn more tasks than in smaller settings with only one. States Wide at times had only one while Urban Center, the largest department, had six.

THE STORE

When he arrives at a store, an apprentice is trained to perform a task, usually working the automatic wrapping machine. If he handles this competently, he is kept there until another apprentice comes. If none comes, he may do this job for years almost without interruption. If a new apprentice comes, he trains him to wrap and then learns another task himself. During busy periods in the department, he may return to the wrapping machine to assist the new man.

In very large meat departments, as many as three apprentices wrap meat while others do something else. But very few cut and saw meat, the journeyman's chief work.

Locale is another dimension. Trying to make a profit usually leads supermarkets to respond to their surroundings. They try to make their wares attractive to consumers in the neighborhood. Different levels of income mean different kinds of meat. T-bone steaks do not sell in poor neighborhoods, nor neck bones and salt pork in wealthy suburbs. Stores offer the kind of meat customers in their locale will buy.

In poor neighborhoods, apprentices have more opportunity to practice cutting meat than in wealthy neighborhoods. Most customers of Urban Local have low incomes. Meat cutters prepared a variety of low-priced cuts, and apprentices could learn on some of the meat with little financial loss to the store. A journeyman explained:

> We let them saw the pork and stuff like that. That's cheap. It doesn't matter if you throw it away. . . . Now the red stuff [he gestured

toward the beef] that's too expensive. We can't throw any of that away. If we let them touch that we watch them very very closely. Usually I saw the beef.

The store prepares large amounts of meat with a much lower wholesale price than beef—chicken, variety meats, salt pork, neck bones, and inexpensive cuts of pork. A miscut on salt pork goes unnoticed, but a miscut on a Delmonico steak can readily be calculated. In Urban Local, the meat department sells so much inexpensive fresh fish that there is a separate counter for it; the wholesale cost of fish is so low that the whole operation of ordering, storing, preparing, selling, and wrapping it is handled by one apprentice. If he makes even a large error in ordering, the loss is not great. He has important tasks every day and does things most apprentices never do.

In higher-income neighborhoods, most of the meat cut is beef, veal, and lamb—all higher in wholesale price than pork. Mistakes with this meat are too costly to risk on an apprentice. One Urban market with an exclusive clientele has no apprentices because, as a journeyman there said, "You don't train an apprentice on aged prime beef" (Urban Fancy). While stores in wealthier areas sell some cheap products. these make up a small proportion of total sales. Journeymen cut expensive beef and lamb on the automatic saw; when there are a few soup bones or pieces of salt pork to cut, it interrupts their routine too much to give the task to an apprentice.

Volume of business is another dimension that affects learning. Metropolitan area meat departments were organized to produce a large volume of a standard product—cuts of meat prepared exactly to the company specification. A division of labor among a relatively large number of workers increases efficiency. Each worker does one or two tasks in the occupational bundle. In this situation, not only apprentices but journeymen, too, seldom learn the full range of tasks once proper to their trade.

TURKISH COMPARISONS

After finishing fieldwork in the Midwest, I was fortunate to be able to broaden my understanding by studying butchers' apprentices in Turkey.[3] There, meat markets handle a much smaller volume, and there is no distant company to supply the meat. Instead, the owner himself goes to the slaughterhouse each morning to bargain for animals. While he is away, his apprentice, usually a son or nephew, does all the work in the shop, including selling to customers. He has probably visited the store as a child and begins work knowing a lot about the bundle of tasks in the occupation. He has a general impression of how the work goes, how to learn the trade, and he already knows his teacher well.

Since most markets have only one room, nothing can be hidden from an apprentice, although in shops with more than one, he may not work at all tasks. Wealthy neighborhoods demand more varieties of cut; apprentices in such stores learn more about meat cutting than in poor neighborhoods, where customers ask for only a few. He learns still more by cutting meat to the customer's order, rather than to a company standard, as in American supermarkets. But he seldom learns how to select and bargain for animals at the slaughterhouse until he owns his own shop. Just as anxious to learn all tasks in the occupational bundle as those in the Midwest, Turkish apprentices had much more chance to do so, yet did not learn them all.

CONCLUSION

Most organizations represent a compromise between the needs and purposes of the various participants. In those where some participants are there to learn, we expect conflict of purpose. Usually educational goals come last.

Many other dimensions—size, physical layout, locale, and volume of trade—affect how many tasks in the bundle apprentices learn. It seems probable that such structural dimensions may be relevant to other situations in which both working and learning take place.

NOTES

1. The discussion is based on participant observation in five supermarket meat departments of varying sizes located in neighborhoods of varying income levels.
2. Store names are pseudonyms.
3. This discussion is based on observation and interviews in seven butcher shops of varying sizes which were located in neighborhoods of varying income levels in a Turkish city. I am grateful to Gülderen Suzek for interpreting the interviews and to the Council for Intersocietal Studies of Northwestern University for lessons in Turkish.

REFERENCE

HUGHES, E. C. (1951) "Studying the nurse's work." Amer. J. of Nursing 51 (May): 294-295.

Situational Learning
in a School with Clients

MARILYN S. NOTKIN
The Hahnemann Medical College and Hospital Unit
Philadelphia, Pennsylvania

Everett Hughes (1958) writes of work that does something *for* or *to* people. In this paper, I show how beauty school students change from "doing to" to "doing for" a patron—a gradual shift of emphasis from exclusive concern with technique to recognition of the importance of the client. This change of definition emerges as students begin work on real clients and learn situationally rather than by precept. In what follows I try to make clear what I mean by situational learning.

Privately owned, the beauty school is one of five in a medium-sized town. It draws students from an area of one hundred miles. On the second floor of a downtown building, the large classroom is filled with stations—working areas, backed with mirrors with chairs in front of them. Stations line the walls, forming a corridor up the center of the room. One portion of the classroom is a beauty salon for advanced students.

EARLY TRAINING

The school admits students at the beginning of every month,[1] with largest enrollment in July and September. There are three regular instructors and weekly sessions with the owner and another male instructor. Patrons of the salon come and go hourly.

The course merges conventional schooling with apprenticeship. There are classes, lectures, and written work but students practice on patrons much like apprentices.

Beginning students regard hairdressing as a matter of mastering certain techniques. The course is an exciting experience. Surroundings are unfamiliar, the routine unknown, equipment complicated. Each student has a textbook, a workbook, and a kit of scissors, combs, and other tools, In a few days, each receives a manikin or "dolly." An expensive model of a woman's head with a full head of hair, the manikin clamps to a swivel mounted at each station. Students use it in all early training and throughout the course.

The first weeks of training are filled with details. Students learn the use and care of equipment and the many rules of the school. There is written material to cover and lectures to attend. There are fumbling efforts to set the manikin's hair and long periods of waiting while the instructor checks other students' work. Students define only working on the dolly as learning. Waiting, listening, reading, and studying are time-fillers between periods of action. Everything that happens in the first weeks reinforces students' belief in the importance of technique.

The instructors do not share the students' view. In the first lecture, major emphasis is on patrons. The instructor states this philosophy: "Every woman has the right to beauty whether she is someone with a problem or whether she is naturally gorgeous." He follows with specifics:

> These clients want to be babied, pampered, spoiled, waited on. These small services won't cost you anything more, but it makes them feel something special and they like it. It is important to know the names of customers, husbands, children, their occupation, likes and dislikes, their good and bad points. . . . Look at her face, take her apart and tell her honestly what kind of things are needed.

Some patrons must be persuaded to accept the operator's authority:

I train my customers. They have a new hairstyle every week. It is not necessary to wear the same style, every week, every year. It's not good for them. If the customer asks why I tell them they need variety, rejuvenation, to get out of their rut, it's good for the scalp. . . . I tell them to consider the people who have to look at them.[2]

These precepts are the beginning of the school's effort to develop a "professional" approach[3] in its students. In time, they accept this instructor's point of view, although at first it seems merely didactic.

Although the school has a well-devised system of procuring patrons, relatives or friends are the students' first patrons. Most students have had some experience with hairdressing before entering school. They report having "done" relatives' hair, sometimes for years. They have experimented with cutting, bleaching, and coloring, as well as setting hair. The announcement that they must supply a model causes little concern.

It is a surprise when things do not work out as anticipated. Mothers are especially difficult: "Now trim, it, Ruthie. I don't need to have it up to my ears. You know what I mean by trim. Have you learned 'trim' yet, Honey?"

Students with more self-reliance also run into trouble:

I was cutting my mother's hair. She had it bleached and it was growing out. All the ends were split and dry and frizzy. . . . I really had to cut those off. . . . But she didn't want it that short. . . . I said, "All right then, I just won't invite you back." And she said, "Well, it's just as well because I wouldn't come back anyway."

This student takes technical responsibility for the patron's hair. It is worth risking her mother's displeasure (but just barely, as she tearfully reported to me later) to do what she has learned is right.

The nervousness the girls exhibit is not merely the stage fright of a first performance. Their situation is transitional. At home in the kitchen with newspapers on the floor to catch hair clippings and instructions for the home permanent spread out on the table, mother may still dominate the interaction. In school the girl is responsible to her instructor and conscious of fellow students observing her behavior as she observes theirs. She knows the patron's hair is her responsibility.

After this experience, students are in increasingly frequent contact with clients. Junior students work on customers called "research clients"—patrons willing to be worked on by an inexperienced student without charge. The students' work is slow and unsure. Their presentation of self is equally uncertain and they do little to mask their discomfort. Reflecting on the early days of her training, a student said:

> Do you know who the worst ones are? They are the ones who come in for research and who get the stuff all free. . . . They're the hardest to deal with because they sit down and they tell you exactly what they want you to do and how to do it. They're the ones that'll pick up the comb and start combing their own hair.

Students learn more from research clients than they do from working on mothers, as it becomes clear that control of interaction with clients must come before technical responsibility for their hair can be achieved. Failure to establish authority gives the patron a chance to dominate. When this happens, an inexperienced student is powerless to reassert herself. She calls on the instructor for help and complains about her customer to fellow students.

WORK ON THE PATRONS

Up to now I have discussed students' educational experiences as if they occurred in orderly sequence. Early in the training, this was true. Taught as a group, the class lunched at the same time and moved from activity to activity together. This lasted only a few days. After work began on patrons, to impose an ordered sequence on their learning would present a false picture. Order continues in the course as devised by the school. An outline designed to assure that students pass the state board examination is followed closely. Instructors teach additional procedures to keep the girls up to date. But what students learn comes increasingly from experiences shared with fellow students. Others' successes and discouragements, fights and frustrations, ambitions and expectations are part of students' development. The shoulds and should nots of technique and the oughts and ought nots of dealing with patrons are constantly shared.

I call this loosely structured interaction, fostered by the open school setting, situational learning. Admission at different times of the year means that students at all levels of training can observe each other. Moreover, the spatial arrangements of the school give visual access to whatever goes on. Most of the instruction, practice, and work on patrons is done in one large work area. There are mirrors everywhere.

Conversation is almost equally available. Background music muffles the clatter, making conversation easy to overhear. A partition separates the salon from the work area but it, too, is accessible to all.

About halfway through the course, classwork is discontinued and students spend most of their time on patrons. Instructors teach by circulating around the room, observing, making comments, cautioning, and complimenting. A teacher may call together a small group and point out some problem or speak to only one girl. Either way, nearby students overhear. Interviewing a girl after graduation, I asked if her training had stressed the importance of getting along with patrons: "We got a lot of instruction about how you can't snap at patrons or that you should act this way or that way. . . . It was woven in with everything."

Teaching is no longer separated from action, as in the early lectures. Instructors tell students how to act with patrons on the spot as work on the patron is about to begin:

> Get your clippies ready, because this will save you time. It's good always to have your tools ready when you're beginning to do a project. Have them laid out nicely and neatly so you don't have them getting in your way. It makes a nice appearance for your patron.

The impression should be maintained:

> Now, girls, remember your posture, don't get in the habit of
> slumping. Always be conscious of your posture and also the motion
> of your hands. You look more professional every day when you are
> aware of these things. And also the expression on your face. Your
> customers will respond to a pleasant face.

Such advice becomes easier to follow as students' skills increase.
Haircuts, sets, and permanents no longer require reference to
charts or instructions and frequent successful contact with
clients contribute to students' belief in their ability to please.
At least part of the time, students can put technique aside and
look to the future—a future in which patrons will have central
importance.

Recognition of the patron's importance changes students'
views of work. No longer something technical that one person
(operator) does to another (patron), work has become an
interaction: what each person does seriously affects the other.
This linkage is implicit in students' conversation among themselves.

Each time a student says a patron "should know," "shouldn't
do," or "ought to allow something," she implies something
about beauty operators as well. Thus: *A patron should know
enough to be on time for appointments.* The more patrons an
operator can serve in a day, the better pleased her employer will
be with her work and the more money she can make. *A patron
shouldn't get angry with the girls.* The girls are students and
cannot be expected to perform as professionals. *A patron ought
to allow the student to use her judgment about the client's hair.*
Students have had months of training and know better than
customers what is good for them.

The rules for clients are strict; those students make for
themselves less so. Sometimes it is expedient to be students,
other times to see themselves as fully qualified, wage-earning
beauty operators. Perspectives in school are transitional—tai-
lored to fit both school and work.

PROFESSIONALISM

Students' increased awareness of the importance of inter-action with patrons manifests itself in the questions they ask. An instructor demonstrating a permanent wave suggests conversational approaches to a patron during the lengthy procedure. An advanced student asks:

> What do you do if you're with a patron and you ask them questions about themselves and their family and what they did over the weekend and they just answer "yes," "no," "mmm," and don't carry on the conversation? The instructor replied, "Well, you take your cue from them. If you ask them a couple of questions and they don't seem inclined to answer, you just keep quiet. But you try to start out at least giving them an opportunity to talk and showing an interest in them because people like that."

To be professional means more than taking technical responsibility for patrons' hair and a pleasing presentation of self. Work is interactional in the fullest sense: clients are people, not just heads of hair; they have personal likes and dislikes the operator must respect.

But the operator must decide whether the patron-as-person has priority over the beautician's responsibility for her hair. An element of risk exists during permanent waving, bleaching, or dyeing even for healthy hair. Damaged hair increases risk and the operator's anxiety:

> [Donna:] I wish you'd look at my hands, how they're trembling. I tell you I'm so nervous about that woman I don't know what to do. Did you see her hair? It's in terrible condition. I told her she shouldn't have a permanent, that her hair might break off—I even made her sign a release . . . but she said, "Well that's all right, go ahead anyway." . . . She must have done that dye job herself. . . . Boy, you can really damage your hair. Apparently she doesn't even care.

Professionalism demands that even irresponsible patrons receive good care. But instructors make the limits of this philosophy clear. A student explains:

Did you hear about Carol? She had this impossible patron. I mean, she was a real bitch and she had Carol in tears. Miss T. came over and she told that patron off. She said that the woman was to remember that she was being taken care of by a student and that students weren't to be talked to like that. If she didn't like it she could go somewhere else. She really stood up for Carol.

Pleasing the patron makes work easier and increases tips, but there are indignities students need not suffer; the school (or employer, as my interviews confirm) will support them.

At times, getting along with people in the open setting of the school demands more self-control than students have. Being on stage almost all the time is unnerving. Emotional outbursts affect students witnessing them. One day a girl burst into the student lounge, talking as she entered, using her hands and arms to express rage at another student.

Shall I tell you what she did to me? I was thinning with the thinning shears for the first time. So maybe I wasn't doing a good job, but you know, I'm here, I'm a student, I'm learning, and she hasn't been here any longer than I have. She says, "Is that the first time you've used thinning shears? You're sure making a mess of it." Now she's saying this and my customer's sitting right there. How do you suppose this is going to make the customer feel . . . like she's being used as a guinea pig. Isn't that a good way to get a tip? And she makes me feel like an idiot in front of my customer. I was ready to kill her.

Even in school, this student feels that professionalism extends beyond interaction with clients to interaction with fellow workers. Beauty operators must protect each other and not do things that spoil their image of themselves or their public image as a group.

Economic advancement becomes important to students nearing the end of the course and about to begin work. The base pay beauty operators earn from their employer is usually low; tips often amount to considerably more. Protecting this source of income is important, and so are steady customers. Some girls had this gratifying experience as students.

Connie entered the lounge with a slip for Betty [indicating a waiting patron]. Betty looked at the slip and said, "Oh, it's Miss B." Connie: "A request?" Betty: "Yes, she always asks for me when she comes in." Connie: "I have a couple who ask for me too. I like that. It gives me a chance to try different things on the same person. And besides, it's nice to be asked for."

To be asked for by clients is to join an elite group of students with high status in the eyes of fellow students, even instructors. After graduation these girls will develop a clientele, a desirable asset to employers. A girl usually takes clients with her if she changes shops, assuring the new employer additional customers and a continued source of income for herself.

CONCLUSION

To summarize, most students enter school believing that to develop technical skills is to learn to work. Starting with their first patron, students redefine what work is.

They discuss with feeling such things as creativity as a quality necessary for good beauty operators, the ethics of giving a woman an unbecoming hairstyle because she asked for it, and whether a beautician must set an example to the world by always looking her best. Their interests are not confined to the technical aspects of the work, nor to making money. Many see themselves as entering a profession—one that offers a degree of independence and requires responsibility.

If the development of this kind of identification with work is a measure of a successful training program, the course is successful despite the absence of several characteristics stressed by educators. The curriculum is not innovative; there is rote learning. At times students' dissatisfaction borders on hostility; they feel the school exploits their services to paying patrons. Yet the amount of discipline they accept is astonishing.

What makes the school a success, in addition to the high quality of the technical training, is the close correspondence between school and work—what I have called situational learning. With slight modifications, perspectives developed in training are those used later at work. The open learning setting permits students to share experiences. They learn from the mistakes and successes of other students as well as from their own. At work on paying patrons, they take risks, but receive protective supervision from instructors who fit precept immediately to practice.

NOTES

1. This study started in September and followed a group of about 25 students through their training. Follow-up interviews were conducted with most students after they had graduated and had been working for several months.

2. As a researcher, I was not exempt from this pressure. Students succeeded in effecting a change in my hairstyle; the first in ten years, and high time, they said.

3. I use the world "professional" as instructors and students used it. For a discussion of the term as an honorific rather than a social category, see Becker (1962).

REFERENCES

BECKER, H. S. (1962) "The nature of profession," pp. 27-46 in Part I of N. B. Henry (ed.) The Sixty-Second Yearbook of the National Society for the Study of Education. Chicago: Univ. of Chicago Press.

HUGHES, E. C. (1958) Men and Their Work. New York: Free Press.

Learning To Sell Door to Door

Teaching as Persuasion

ROBERT BOGDAN

Center on Human Policy, Department of Special Education
Syracuse University

Much human interaction is persuasion. Door-to-door salesmen use it more consciously than other occupational groups, their training courses make persuasive techniques explicit. In this paper, I examine sales training with data from two direct sales training programs held in a middle-sized northeastern city.

Both one-week courses were sponsored by the sales division of national firms with standarized marketing schemes. I attended all training sessions, accompanied trainees on their first calls, and learned about the courses, as trainees did, by responding to classified ads. One company sold encyclopedias; the other vacuum cleaners.

THE SCRIPT

On the first day of class, trainees receive a booklet. The instructor says, "This is the script ... you'll be expected to commit it to memory." The script, "canned talk" or "spiel," is central to the course. It outlines what the salesman says to the client from the moment he knocks on the door until he leaves, and it takes an hour to present.

At first memorizing the script seems an impossible task, but instructors assure trainees, "Everyone has trouble doing memory work—all it takes is a lot of practice." Much practice follows. Students present the script to the class; they present it to family and friends; they hear the instructor recite it over and over again.

Rather than memorize it verbatim, trainees learn the sequence of topics, major points, and some of the wording. Instructors encourage modifications: "change the sentence structure slightly to fit you own personality and your own way of speaking."

Trainees prompt each other when they make mistakes. The instructor points out key phrases to learn to make remembering easier. He shows trainees how to use the product in conjunction with the script. Tangible items provide hooks on which to hang sections of the presentation. He breaks the script down into named sections. For the encyclopedia company, the pitch refers to the entire presentation. It is broken down into the front talk, small talk, pamphlet talk, the advertising campaign, the qualifier, the demonstration, and the close.

The script is a strategy in itself, a written guide for interaction with the client, assuring the salesman of continuity in his presentation and exact knowledge of what comes next. One idea flows into another; he need never worry about transitions nor be at a loss for words. Knowing precisely what he is going to say, the trainee gains confidence that he can persuade the client to buy.

The instructor performs the script expressively. He names the clients Mr. and Mrs. Jones; two students act the parts.

Students' first recitals are bland. The instructor urges them to smile, lean over the client's shoulder, use their hands, look him right in the eye. Playing all parts at once—salesman, client, and himself—he interrupts himself to explain a gesture, the wording of a sentence, or the psychology of what he is doing. As salesman, "Isn't that a fantastic offer? Isn't it Mrs. Jones? Isn't it Mr. Jones?" and then walks over to the student playing Mrs. Jones with pen in hand.

Instructors tell many stories about salesmen's encounters with clients. Told in great detail, the tales create client types. Of a Ph.D. in psychology with cats, a filthy house, and no children: "Their house was as clean as they wanted it. . . . You can't sell people like that." But some clients are a surprise:

> I was bending down. . . . I wasn't too interested in what Mr. and Mrs. Jones were doing. I looked up and saw them. Hell, they were raising off their chairs like Siamese twins . . . listening to every word I said. You can't tell—you get those people who yes you up and down: "This is wonderful. . . . What a wonderful plan" and then don't buy. You get the *slowcomers.* They're not saying much but they're digesting everything. . . . So don't let up if . . . they're not doing a toe dance around the room for you.

Clients who know too much make "static" (resist the pitch):

> This one man, hell of a nice fella, went out on his first call. It was the house of a G.E. engineer . . . he really gave the demonstrator a hard time. . . . Asked questions about the motor.

Each trainee goes out early in the training program with an experienced salesman. He returns full of customer stories for fellow trainees:

> The night I went out with him [salesmanager] we drove into this driveway. There was this man standing there working on his garden. Howard lifted his hand, waved at the guy and said, "Good evening." The guy got this big smile on his face, raised his hand and waved. Howard looked at me and says, "This asshole is sold, get out the contract." He sold him too.

A clear typology of clients cannot be drawn from these stories. According to one instructor, "When you're in this business for a while you get cynical about people. You meet enough of them and you begin to think they're pretty stupid." Another says, "People are nice and friendly and want to hear what you have to say." Clients are easy to persuade (nice or stupid) or deserve to be persuaded (bastards or assholes). Both definitions ease interaction.

LINING UP THE CLIENTS

While stories will do for general information, instructors give trainees detailed instruction in "sizing up" clients. No salesman wants to waste time giving a complete presentation to clients unlikely to buy. The presentation should fit the client from the start. Sizing up enables him to withdraw early or modify his presentation.

The vacuum cleaner company checks the credit ratings of potential clients called by telephone and refers only those in good financial standing to salesmen. Encyclopedia salesmen go out "cold canvassing," and rely on observation to choose a door. Toys and children on the lawn are positive signs; clients buy for their children. Run-down houses suggest low buying power. New salesmen seem to avoid expensive homes. A modest house assures them they will not be overmatched educationally or socially.

In the preliminary stages of the encyclopedia presentation, salesmen engage the client in apparently casual conversation, designed to uncover the client's buying potential. This method of sizing up is called "small talk." Here a student plays Mr. Jones and the instructor interrogates him:

Q: This is a nice section of town. Fine house you have here, Mr. Jones. Are you the owner?
A: No.
Q: Oh, I see, you're leasing it, then.
A: That's right.
Q: It certainly is a very fine place, Mr. Jones, I have an old friend by that name, really a nice feller. He's an engineer. That wouldn't happen to be your line of work would it?
A: No, I'm a salesman.
Q: Well, that's a demanding line of work. They must keep you pretty busy.

The instructor explains the phrase "they must keep you pretty busy":

> now chances are if he's been out of work on illness, or on strike or if he's unemployed, he's going to tell you about it. . . . He might tell you that he . . . broke his back and was out of work. . . . You don't have time to waste. There's a door right up the block where the man's been busy all year.

Instructors and company officials believe people are leery of door-to-door salesmen. "Lining up" and "getting in" are techniques designed to overcome this resistance. In the vacuum cleaner sales program, trainees learn two methods of lining up—an oblique approach and a direct one. The oblique approach misrepresents the purpose of the initial contact. A secretary at the company office picks names at random from the local telephone directory. She plays a recording:

> You are one of the lucky persons who have been selected to receive a free gift as part of our new advertising campaign. In order to receive your attractive gift you must call the following number within the next ten minutes.

If the party calls, she says one of the company's advertising representatives will deliver the gift to his home. She sets up an appointment and a salesman makes the delivery.

The instructor tells trainees how to get in after the client has been lined up by telephone:

> go up, knock on the door, smile and say, "Good evening Mr. Jones. My office called this morning and made an appointment with your wife. . . . I have a free gift for you out in my car. I'll go get it and be back in a minute." Now Mr. Jones is standing right in the doorway waiting to receive it, you go out, get the [demonstration] equipment and you walk up to the door. There's Mr. Jones holding it open for you.

A direct method of lining up is an advertising club. Vacuum cleaner buyers are eligible for membership. They turn in names of friends and relatives; for each couple seeing a complete home demonstration, the club member receives five dollars. Getting in is assured.

GETTING IN THE DOOR

Lining up clients and getting in is more difficult for the encyclopedia salesman. After knocking on the door, he uses an oblique approach: he says he is visiting in the neighborhood to inform people about a new teaching machine. The teaching machine arouses clients' interest and the salesman enters as an educator.

In the oblique approach, the salesman gets in on spurious grounds that do not lead directly to a sale. The salesman who presents himself falsely must make a transition from the front used in lining up and getting in to one more related to his objective. Handled incorrectly, the client becomes alarmed. To make the transition from educator to book salesman, trainees memorize a bridge-phrase: "I represent the manufacturers of the teaching machine. . . . You probably know us better as the publishers of the world famous Encyclopedia ——."

The instructor tells students:

> Now this is a tricky transition. . . . You think that when you reveal to them that you're associated with a book firm, Mr. Jones is going to hit the ceiling. That's not true. . . . That doesn't mean that he's not going to get somewhat shook. The next sentence is: "However, I do want to set your mind at ease. I'm not in your home this evening to interest you in the direct purchase of any of our products. That's not my job. I'm here for a much more important reason. To get the use of your name."

The advertising campaign talk follows.

Once the vacuum cleaner salesman is in the door, he presents a small gift and says, "In return for this fine gift I am sure you won't mind answering a few questions; if they're not of a personal nature, that is." The questions lead into the demonstration. Here the salesman appeals to clients' sense of fair play. Answers repay the gift.

SELLING TECHNIQUES

A front is an impression of himself a man fosters in others by his posture, speech, facial expression, gestures, and dress. There are standard fronts corresponding to various statuses in society; the actor in a given status uses the front proper to his status. A man representing himself as something he is not uses a false front. Teaching the false front is an important part of training. Companies believe the public imputes foul play to salesmen. Presenting himself as a salesman starts a man off with a strike against him.

You're not there to sell. . . . You're part of the advertising division. As salesman: "What, me sell books? Ridiculous, I wouldn't do that. It's below me. I'm a high position executive in the advertising division out organizing a new sales program." It is very important that you get that in your mind. You're a member of the advertising division. Throughout the night you have to act that way.

Trainees are coached to "use short sentences. You look at your watch. Your time is important to you . . in that way, you've established your own importance."

White socks, sideburns, or mustaches "don't go with the image . . . you'll come off as a con man." Certain words are forbidden: sale, scheme, buy, cost, and price.

Don't say deal! People don't like to hear that. They think you're trying to put something over on them. We don't want people to think that we're wheelers and dealers. . . . We don't have any deals, remember that, fellers. . . . We have wonderful programs, a terrific machine, but we don't have any deals.

The front must seem sincere. Trainees must use gestures, facial expression, and tones of voice that transmit a feeling they can be trusted.

"Assuming the sale" is implicit in the script. The salesman treats the client as if he is going to buy. The technique obligates the client. Before mentioning the contract trainees say: "The bookcase comes in either a maple finish as illustrated here or in a blond finish. Now with the decor of this room, I would suggest the darker wood. What do you think?"

"Yes, yes, yes" is a technique that makes the client affirm what the salesman says or praise the product.

— Isn't that right, Mrs. Jones?
— Now, isn't that a wonderful program.
— You'll agree it's a terrific machine?

Dale Carnegie (1937) explains the forced affirmative as avoiding negative response. This moves the client toward a mood of acceptance difficult to change at the point of decision.

During training, instructor and script direct trainees to get the client actively involved. Have clients touch the vacuum cleaner, feel the paper in the encyclopedia, get them talking. "They'll wind up selling themselves."

"Getting the client involved" is similar to yes, yes, yes. By cooperating, the client becomes obligated to remain so and sign the contract.

Control of the client is a conscious sales strategy. Because he has given the presentation many times and memorized the script, the trainee knows what to do, while the client is often ill at ease. Putting clients at ease helps the sale. One instructor knocks on the kitchen door:

> There you are in a cozy little space with lots of room to lay out your materials. . . . There's something about the hominess and warmth of the kitchen which is conducive to sales. . . . You're setting the stage so it's advantageous to you.

The emphasis on control fosters confidence—as important a part of training as learning specific techniques.

Buying the product is presented as a noble act. Trainees must tell clients that parents who buy are intelligent, future-oriented, and happy. They value education and love their children. Living up to this model means purchasing the books.

The salesman establishes the credibility of his company.

Testimonials, repeated association with well-known products, noted authorities, and institutions make this point.

Finally, trainees learn a positive attitude toward memorizing the script and selling.

Instructor: "OK, Ernie, are you ready to give it a try" [recite the script]? Ernie: "Ready, willing, but I don't know how able." Instructor: "That's the spirit that I like to see. That's the only kind of spirit you can have in this business. If you're gonna strike out [not make a sale], what the hell. . . . It's better to have tried and failed than not to have tried at all. Give 'em hell, Ernie."

Joking is common. While putting materials in an attaché case for a trainee making his first call, the instructor said, "Art, you think four contracts are enough for you tonight or do you think you'll write more? I'll play it safe and give you six." After a student completed his recital, the instructor said, "That's very good, Charlie. You'll write two [orders] tonight." Charlie said, "Only two?"

Developing the proper attitude to handle fear is part of training. Trainees' nervousness before their first calls is obvious. Instructors attempt to ward it off. One instructor described his first experience selling door-to-door in detail. He dramatized how his knees knocked as he knocked on the client's door. In both courses, all trainees go out on their first calls on the same night. In the office getting their assignments, they encourage each other and get pep talks from the staff.

CONCLUSION

As I observed the program, I realized students' experience selling techniques to persuade them to join the company and participate fully in the training program. Ads run in the local paper line up potential trainees. Both companies misrepresent the job, not mentioning selling or the name of the company. The encyclopedia company's ad speaks of learning to demonstrate teaching machines. The men learn it is a course in selling only when they arrive and find a class assembled. The company's credibility is stressed. Its representative, the teacher, promotes selling by an appeal to the noble.

> Life is a sacrifice and you are going to have to believe that. I'm working behind that desk 16 hours a day. . . . Why am I there? Because I'm the kind of guy who wants to give my wife and children the kinds of things they deserve. I can't stand to see them in need. . . . If you haven't come to the point in your life when you say, hell I'm not the only person, if you haven't lost this selfishness and don't have the concern of your family at heart, I don't think you're much of a man.

Assuming the sale is also used. Potential trainees are not asked whether they will attend the course; they choose one of two scheduled times. The effectiveness of the script is an important selling point, driven home by forcing trainees to yes, yes, yes. Trainees soon begin saying, "You get that down and you can't miss . . . the script is real good." Instructors dilate on their own successful selling years, introduce company salesmen who "made it big," and display their sales records. Each trainee goes out with the salesmanager, an expert who often "connects" (makes a sale). Sale or not, trainees return with tales about how Mr. Blank had the client eating out of his hand.

Full of confidence, the trainee, with his equipment in his car and the training sessions behind him, drives away from the company office to knock on that first door. Has he been sold? Whatever the result, his experience suggests we reexamine training and teaching as persuasive arts.

REFERENCES

CARNEGIE, D. (1937) How to Win Friends and Influence People. New York: Simon & Schuster.
GOFFMAN, E. (1959) The Presentation of Self in Everyday Life. New York: Doubleday Anchor.

Individuality in a Factory

ESTHER YOUNG
Department of Sociology
Syracuse University

The consequences in boredom, fatigue, and meaninglessness for individuals engaged in mass-producing interchangeable parts of products have been extensively dealt with in sociology (Marx, 1956; Blauner, 1964; Seeman, 1959; Faunce, 1968; Friedmann, 1961). Weil's (1962: 455) comments are typical:

> At the worker level, the relations established among various jobs and functions are relationships between things, not men. The parts circulate with labels bearing their name, material and degree of elaboration; one could almost believe that they are the persons, and the workers the interchangeable parts.

Less frequently treated[1] is the question: Does some meaning remain despite boredom and fatigue? If there is a residue, what is its source? What consequences does it have?

While gathering data on workers' experiences learning new jobs in an electronics plant, I found a residue of meaning and learned something of its sources and consequences. I observed women on two nonmoving lines assembling small components and employees in a three-day retraining course. Throughout the plant, workers moved often from one station to another and to new lines and buildings as lines shut down and workers without seniority were "bumped" down the line. Learning a new job was a common experience; employees frequently discussed their moves and relearning. Their talk exposed some of the persisting meaning of factory work.

Meanings are people's interpretations of social and natural events. Often taken for granted, they emerge from diverse social and mental processes and include seeing oneself and one's experiences as objects. One compares these objects with past experience and imagined futures[2] and the evaluations of others.[3] The latter, more social aspect of meaning, approximates group definition. Meanings are thus analytically separable from (although related to) situational definitions shared with others.

INPUTS OF MEANING

Selectivity and emphasis mark the meanings individuals and groups hold, and these qualities have long intrigued sociologists. How is it, they ask, that what seems to be a circumstance calling for an obvious explanation is so often interpreted illogically? To find answers, researchers sort out from a larger totality, the significant elements of the situation—what it means to those in it. In my study of workers' experiences, I considered a host of circumstances—tasks, machines, fellow workers, inspectors, foremen, the front office, group definitions regarding which rules to keep and which to break, job-ratings and pay scale, methods of training, ideas about sex differences, and production quotas. I wondered if any meaning persisted for individuals beyond boredom and fatigue. Workers' feelings while learning to make interchangeable lookalikes suggested an answer.

Although looking alike does not guarantee that electronic components are alike—i.e., will test and perform alike—inspectors prefer lookalikes to products expressing individuality. The idiosyncratic component may not fit well with other components when assembled. Compact design demands that a lead-wire be precisely placed to allow its neighbors space. A performance criterion requires that only certain parts make connections, while others must keep clear of one another to avoid short circuits. A scratch on a printed circuit, a kink or improper bend in a wire, too big a glob of solder, a loose and slack crimp, and too small a cut in insulation suggest trouble. Such visibly detectable mistakes are easily caught by inspectors who discard the part or return it to the maker who has not produced an interchangeable lookalike. Neither worker nor product may express individuality, one might conclude, but this would leave out learning.

Line workers refer to learning a new job as "getting the hang of it," a phrase that suggests variability. As one teacher said,[4]

> There are really many ways of doing the same thing. No one way has to be *the* right way. Just as long as everything comes out looking the same, we don't care how people do it. If they have their own way and it looks all right when they are finished, that's fine with us.

Workers share the view that some things cannot be taught; each man must find his own way of doing a given task. As Sigrid, a conscientious worker, explained:

> Nobody told me this, I just learned it myself. When I first came everybody showed me their own way of doing it and I still couldn't get it right and then finally I found a way that I could do.

A meaning-imputing, meaning-invoking individual has expressed her individuality while producing an interchangeable lookalike. Mass production challenges the worker to become conscious of the nature of her performance.

It is likely that the meaning of learning a new task never totally disappears from the worker's definition of factory work. When business is bad or good, workers change stations; they are bumped or promoted. A new station usually demands learning new skills. As they learn new tasks or observe others learn, workers recall how they learned to "do it my own way," and meaning accumulated during learning is reinforced.

This meaning-residue may help mass producers to survive the

monotony of their work. Going to sleep at a machine is uncommon but not unheard of. Women fall forward on the machine and wake themselves. Some sing, apparently to relieve boredom. Such jobs are not "interesting," but some women say they like their work. Others like the financial benefits. All impute meaning to the job and survive, not by adjusting to it but by constructing new meanings conducive to psychic survival.

Teaching may contribute to the workers' belief that everyone learns his own way of doing a task. In the factory, to teach is to perform an operation while the learner watches. Verbal explanation of movements and how they are made are usually absent. This provides the learner with the opportunity to perceive for herself and (occasionally) articulate what is being done. When she finds this out, she has found her own way of doing the task.

The foreman told Dolores, on her first day at a new station, to "watch" Sigrid, whom she was bumping. During the cigarette break, Sigrid said:

> "Now the most important thing to learning the job is that you've gotta watch what I'm doing." Dolores said, "I think you can't learn a job until you do it yourself awhile." Sigrid insisted, "Well the most important thing is to watch."

Sigrid remembered her own difficulty in learning and thought she was helping Dolores. Nevertheless, she left it largely up to Dolores to discern what she was watching:

> Dolores continued to have difficulty tweeking off the tail of her lead wires and Sigrid said, "Here now, watch this. Look how I do it. Look where I put my tweezers." And Sigrid put her tweezers down with one edge turned at an angle and she quickly twisted off the lead tail. She did not, however, explain what it was that she was doing. Dolores tried a few more and at last she got one where she could tweak off the end.

Until Dolores perceived it was the angle, not *where* Sigrid held the tweezers, she could not do the task. The time it took her to "catch on" she later viewed as the time during which she found her own way of doing it.

Perhaps we tend to think that things done with our hands are external, something to be learned by watching others perform. In the factory, most people eventually learn tasks, and because learners are always told to watch, supervisors and workers alike agree one learns by watching. But however important workers consider such teaching, they 'agree it is insufficient. To master a task, each operator must learn her own way of doing things.

Management believes supervisors or other employees teach operators. Accounting categories have a slot for training time, not learning time. Supervisors charge a worker's first day and a half to training, but, as one production official said:

> "We know that maybe it takes 2 or 3 months for someone to get up to his peak in production, so how much of his first 2 or 3 months ought to be charged to training?" And he shrugged his shoulders.

This uncertainty seldom reaches middle management, although people at the training center suggest it when they say: "After all, we can't teach them everything they need to know in a week." Management's more usual view denies the learner's active role. As one official put it,

> We used to have, say, a silversmith who had a little wad of silver and his two hands and his table and he'd work maybe a day or maybe a week . . . making something out of this silver. . . . When he got finished . . . he would turn it upside down and put his trademark on it. . . . Today employees can't put their trademark on the product. There's one trademark put on it . . . and that is for all of us. . . . What we've lost today is individualism.

GROUP NORMS AND INDIVIDUALITY

The meaning of a production job today is enmeshed in the manufacturing past.[5] A job is what it is not: it is not the kind of job people used to have. Creativity and commitment are lacking. Management's job becomes training individuals to fill jobs that have lost meaning. For workers, jobs are boring, but learning retains personal challenge.

Workers and management also see the time spent mastering a task differently. For management it is a cost; for workers, a coping with the job. Still another dissimilarity leaves workers a residue of meaning not available to management. For the manager, teaching and learning are entwined; for the operator they are separated by a link—or perhaps a gap—that infuses the job with meaning. To fill the gap is to learn one's own way of doing a job.

Furthermore, workers see themselves not as interchangeable, but as different—individually. and according to sex category. Some workers take longer than others to find their own way of doing a job. Experience, natural ability, even physical characteristics explain variations in learning time and quality or quantity of production. Production of lookalikes proceeds despite a widely shared assumption that, although interchanged, individuals differ. As they move from station to station or watch others come and go, workers explain the trouble some have in catching on by individual idiosyncracies.

Those who have no difficulty—the outstanding performers—are examples, but not standard setters, for others. Florence, an inspector and the highest-rated hourly worker on the line, explained:

> Now take Mable. Mable was a fast worker and she got her quota but I wouldn't call Mable's work perfect. I don't know how to explain it but all of hers wouldn't be the same. Now there are some girls who can make every unit look just like every other unit. They get the wire soldered in exactly the same place each time. But now Mable's wouldn't be like that. She'd have maybe one wire up too high and the next wire down too low. It just wasn't what I'd call top quality. Now there are some girls who can really weld like I said. Bill [foreman] always said that Idella who used to be here was the best welder that he's ever seen. . . . I don't think it would have made any difference how long Mable would have been here. I don't think hers would have been any better.

Florence accepted most of what Sigrid produced although all

units did not look alike. Lookalikes are almost alike. Something about workers turns looking alike into an ideal not usually achieved. Individuality is both noted and enhanced. If mass production blocks expression of creativity, it fails to stifle the creation of individuals by themselves and others.

One might ask, however, if group norms limit expressions of individuality. Do workers set maximal limits on production and minimal limits on coffee breaks? The answer is "of course." There are shared understandings on how much to produce: one does not reach the daily quota. If you do, you put extras aside to be counted the next day. And a worker who does not take extra restroom breaks may find the air hose of her machine repeatedly disconnected.

Individuality is built into some shared understandings. For example, less conformity to production-decreasing norms is expected of women than of men. As one steward said, "Of course the women don't stick together like men do. . . . I don't know what it is about women but they just don't stick together." The belief allows female workers further opportunity for a sense of self.

Management treats the sexes differently. The employment center has two waiting areas, one for women, one for men. Women's applications go in one basket, men's in another. All female production employees begin at the basic rate but not all males. Women move to women's jobs with ratings different, in most instances, from men's. The rationale for such differential treatment is that certain tasks require lifting, and labor codes prohibit hiring women for those positions. Lifting may explain why certain jobs are closed to women, but not why men do not, for example, assemble small components. We must turn to something other than public rationale: shared beliefs about jobs appropriate to each sex. As one man said in retraining when shown a film about small tools and circuit boards: "You're kidding. Small tools? Circuit boards? Why, we got girls in our department to do circuit boards. How come we're supposed to do that?"

The belief that some jobs are appropriate to women is

justified by a notion that small hands are dextrous. Jobs demanding dexterity are women's work. Such beliefs and circumstances contribute to the complex of ideas about sex differences that permit women to escape some union demands.

My data indicate men and women differ, or believe they differ, over what an operator may properly do to keep his machine in working condition. Women, people think, make more minor adjustments than men. A foreman explained:

> [if] something went wrong on a machine and it would only take a screwdriver or maybe even just a nailfile or a penny to tighten it a little, a guy would sit there and wait until an electrician or a maintenance man got around to fix it. I'll say this for the women, they are more willing to jump in and help out when they see something needs to be done.

When a machine breaks down, the operator, according to union rules, must call the machine attendant assigned to the line. If he cannot repair it, the toolmaker is called. If this man fails, he calls a specialist. The worker can relax, wisecrack, and gossip in this good company. Accounting procedures subtract time spent during machine breakdowns. Since quotas are proportionate to time actually at work, we might expect employees to take little interest in keeping machines working. But many women provide their own tools for the task.

As James (1968) and Cooley (1968) noted, an individual has several selves, and one is his material self or possessions. In the factory, women express individuality by owning tools. I observed Sigrid open a small plastic case and take out a piece of what looked like emory board.

> You see, you have to keep this cleaned off or it won't work right. Well, now I'm not supposed to even touch my machine. The union says if anything goes wrong with my machine or if I have to do anything to it I'm supposed to call the machine attendant. But look, say you call the machine attendant and he's working at some other machine and he's not going to be done for an hour so you sit there when maybe all you have to do is just do this to it. [She ran the piece of emory board across her machine again.]

Her tools were a piece of green plastic, a bit of transparent tape, an emory board, and tweezers. At the end of the day, she took the kit home.

Sigrid was a good worker, but owning tools is not limited to eager beavers. On another line, components sometimes lodge in the machine because the metal cards that carry them are bent. Some women keep pliers to tug faulty cards through the machine. Workers who do not own pliers borrow them. Watching a woman take pliers from her purse, I asked if she owned other tools:

> She said, "Yes. I've got a kit of little wrenches too." And she put her hand on a small plastic case at the back of her station. I said, "What do you need wrenches for?" She said, "Sometimes your machine gets out of adjustment like up here," and she put her hands on some parts up at the top of her machine and said, "All you've gotta do is adjust it a little and then it's okay again." . . . I asked, "Does the steward care if you fix your machine?" She said, "Oh they don't care if you just make minor adjustments. We call it making minor adjustments."

Unlike men, women have two sets of superordinates at the factory—bureaucratic and sexual. When a boss is a man, the fun of fooling him may double.

There is fragmentary evidence that in spite of the individuality they express by a lack of solidarity, women take the male evaluation of themselves in something akin to self-hatred for such expressions of individuality. "There's nothing worse than a bunch of women" is a woman's phrase. But as with other evaluations (boring jobs), some individuality remains. Negative evaluations contribute to the emergence of persistent meanings in circumstances usually described as meaningless.

CONCLUSION

By way of summary, contemporary mass-producers possess a job-related sense of individuality. What is sensed in self is also perceived as sensed by others. This sense of self is due in part to brief, nonverbal training that lets a worker believe she has found her own way of doing a job. Sharing a definition of women as nonconformers permits further expression of individuality.

NOTES

1. Exceptions are Berger (1964) and the work of Everett Hughes and his students.

2. Alfred Schutz (1967) deals with the self as experiencer. Here I separate the self as learner-experiencer from such phenomena as the circumstances of teaching and social support for the learner's beliefs.

3. Cooley's looking-glass self.

4. At the retraining center, teachers were hourly rated employees promoted to their present jobs. While favorable to management, they still carried the worker-understandings about the necessity of each individual learning his own way of doing a task.

5. Following Husserl and Schutz, Maurice Natanson (1968) looks at how man sees the world of the here and now, but does not consider that the here and now may vary with one's position in the social structure.

REFERENCES

BERGER, P. (1964) The Human Shape of Work. New York: Macmillan.

BLAUNER, R. (1964) Alienation and Freedom. Chicago: Univ. of Chicago Press.

COOLEY, C. H. (1968) "The social self: on the meanings of 'I,' " pp. 87-92 in C. Gordon and K. Gergen (eds.) The Self in Social Interaction. New York: John Wiley.

FAUNCE, W. (1968) Problems of an Industrial Society. New York: McGraw-Hill.

FRIEDMANN, G. (1961) The Anatomy of Work. New York: Free Press.

JAMES, W. (1968) "The self," pp. 41-50 in C. Gordon and K. Gergen (eds.) The Self in Social Interaction. New York: John Wiley.

MARX, K. (1956) Article in T. B. Bottomore (ed.) Selected Writings in Sociology and Social Philosophy. New York: McGraw-Hill.

NATANSON, M. (1968) "Address to the symposium of the Maxwell Graduate School of Public Affairs." Syracuse University Department of Political Science, May 2.

SCHUTZ, A. (1967) The Phenomenology of the Social World. Evanston, Ill.: Northwestern Univ. Press.

SEEMAN, M. (1959) "On the meaning of alienation." Amer. Soc. Rev. 24 (December): 783-791.

WEIL, S. (1962) "Factory work," pp. 452-457 in S. Nosow and W. Form (eds.) Man, Work and Society. New York: Basic Books.

External Control of Recruits

The County Jail School

LEWIS A. MENNERICK
Department of Sociology
University of Kansas

Where it recruits new members and how easy it is to loosen their ties to outside groups have many consequences for any organization. This is especially so for schools, since it is usually their goal to prepare recruits to enter still other groups, often quite foreign to students' earlier lives. At one extreme, schools are in control almost from the start. As in certain religious institutions, they isolate recruits and permit them little contact with outside groups. At the other extreme, students remain under the control of outside organizations and, as a result, the school is subject to numerous external constraints. In this paper I examine one such extreme case, a county jail school.

DESCRIPTION

The school studied is a subsection of Metropolitan County jail. It has many characteristics we normally associate with

Author's Note: *I wish to thank Kenneth C. W. Kammeyer for his comments on an earlier draft and the Metropolitan Board of Education, jail officials, and school personnel (especially the principal) who assisted me greatly. All names, including Metropolitan County Jail, are pseudonyms.*

schools—classrooms, teachers, students, and textbooks. But when we examine its organization more closely, we find the school unique in ways intricately related to its environment (Gross, 1965: 143-147; Olsen, 1968: 21-29; Zald, 1960: 59-62). Constraints imposed on students by the jail itself, the courts, and more generally the city and county in which the jail is located drastically affect the operation of the school. Two features of the relationship are especially salient: the jail's emphasis on custody security rather than treatment (Mennerick, 1971: 114-150) and its control over the school's recruits. Here, I deal with the latter; specifically: how the school copes with a situation in which there is external control over (1) when its students arrive and how long they stay, and (2) what kinds and how many students there are.

Metropolitan County Jail serves a large, northern urban area. Its population, averaging approximately 1,800 prisoners daily, includes both sentenced misdemeanants and nonsentenced inmates awaiting trial. Located in the basement of two cellblocks, the school is staffed by ten full-time teachers and a principal supplied by the board of education. There are four academic classrooms and shops for crafts, wood-working, and printing in the vocational section. School is open year-round, ordinarily for four hours a day, five days a week, with a normal daily enrollment of approximately 150.

The jail assigns all male inmates between seventeen and twenty to the same tiers. The typical tier contains 39 cells, each five by eight feet and built so small as to make it "impossible" to house more than one inmate per cell. Some tiers now house as many as 60 to 70 inmates, and in many cases two inmates share the same cell. Inmates on the school tiers become students. They have no choice. Recruitment is selective only insofar as the police and courts differentially enforce the law.

The jail is a short-term detention facility. The average sentence of convicted misdemeanants in the school section is about three months.

The length of stay on nonsentenced inmates ranges from a few minutes to several months, or an average of 19.5 days.[1]

Since school does not operate on weekends and inmates often spend entire days in court, in the infirmary, or in their cells being disciplined, the number of days spent in classrooms is further reduced. It is impossible for anyone to predict how long nonsentenced students will stay. Some are released from jail before they have been in school. Those enrolled may be released on bail, go to court and be released, or remain in jail indefinitely while their cases are processed. At the very beginning of the study, a jail administrator told me:

> Well, first of all, I want to tell you that the educational program in the jail or in any penal institution is nothing but a whitewash. It's not the fault of the teachers or the principal—for in this jail, they're all good men, all highly qualified. However, it is just too difficult to do anything, with all the turnover and what have you.

Control by the jail over the school's recruiting is complete. The school must take all inmates sent to it and somehow cope with a high rate of turnover in its student population, irregular attendance, and the unpredictable length of each student's stay. In the staff's eyes, these problems affect nearly every aspect of the school's operation—its enrollment and classification procedures, its curriculum, teaching techniques, testing, and grades.

INMATE PROCESSING

When a new inmate comes to the school, a member of the staff interviews him and fills out an enrollment card which includes the last school and grade he attended. A nonsentenced inmate then goes to one of the four academic classrooms—one room for third- and fourth-year high school, another for the first and second years, and two for students with only a grammar school education. Inmates' reports of last grade attended is the basis of classification, even though they sometimes lie.

At times, enrollment procedures are less straightforward. The staff takes such contingencies as the number of students already in a classroom, the inmate's ability to speak English, and his attitude into consideration.

> Then as the [administrator] was about to hand him his enrollment card the boy said, "Sir, could I go to room four?" The [administrator] asked, "Why do you want to go there? What, do you have a friend in there?" The boy answered affirmatively, and the [administrator] said, "Don't start telling us where to put you. That's a good reason for you to be in room two. Take this card and give it to the teacher."

Thus, the school enrolls students without checking previous academic records or doing any formal testing.

Nonsentenced inmates are always assigned to the academic section rather than to vocational training; the uncertain length of their stay disrupts academic classes less than it does the shops. Since the vocational section needs time to acquaint inmates with safety procedures for the various machines and tools, sentenced inmates (usually in school longer and with a more certain length of stay) are customarily assigned to the shops. A vocational teacher told me:

> I think you'll find that there is night and day difference between the sentenced and nonsentenced boys. Of course, part of it has to do with their offenses. Over there [the academic section] you can have everything from murderers to rapists. The sentenced inmates are just here on misdemeanors. They are just generally better. They don't cause so much trouble and can be trusted more. Of course, they have to be trusted if they're going to be allowed to work in a shop like this.

In sharp contrast to the public school system, where it is sometimes looked down upon, vocational training is for the school's better students, those who stay longer and make less trouble.

Teachers in public schools usually prepare lesson plans, a daily and weekly outline of topics to be covered. In the jail school, they practice "bits-and-pieces" teaching. I use this phrase descriptively, not evaluatively, to refer to a situation in which the constraints of the larger system lead teachers to adopt ways of teaching they think at variance with conventional high school methods.

DESCRIPTION OF STUDIES

The primary components of bits-and-pieces teaching are short-term assignments—lessons that can be covered in one or two days—and individual tutoring. The teacher may use such teaching aides as *Junior Scholastic* magazine. Students read a short article and then answer the questions accompanying the article or discuss the material as a class. Teachers also use short sections from standard textbooks in this manner. They have students write spelling words a number of times and then use them in sentences. Any student can begin such an assignment at any time. The class is not disrupted when an inmate leaves and a new one enrolls. A teacher explained:

> Well, this morning we'll be using this magazine. . . . Yesterday, they worked on some exercises in here. Today we'll go over them and correct their answers. You see what we do here isn't anything like in a regular school. The kids are just coming and going too fast.

While teachers differ in emphasis and technique, the following is typical:

> The teacher took three lists from his desk. The first consisted of buildings [the municipal auditorium, the major league ball park, a major bank building, etc.]. He said he would ask students if they knew where these buildings were located and if they had ever been to them. The second was a list of different types of meat. From what animal do we get beef, venison, pork, etc.? He said, "You'd be surprised how many of these guys don't know where most of these places are. Occasionally, you'll get one who knows all of them and has even been to all of them. Most of the guys know where the ball park is and also the municipal auditorium. So you can see, their world is pretty small. . . . In my own way I think that I do help a few of the boys. Most of them are just too far gone, but occasionally you will find one who seems to profit. I think that if I can just help one boy a month, I'm doing well."

Each class sees a movie for about one hour every day or every other day. They include such titles as "Travel in the United States," "Basic Ideas on Gravitation," and "Travel to Argentina." The teacher told me:

> Some of them are elementary science movies. Others of them are about the United States or they are about other countries. I try to teach them something about the relations between various ethnic groups.

Some teachers allow ten or fifteen minutes at the end of the period for students to look at magazines or write letters to friends or family. "You just kind of have to work it out as you go along. I try to find things that will be useful to them and things that they're interested in."

While the class works on one assignment, the teacher may work with a boy on an unrelated topic. The student who gets individual attention is usually either greatly behind or ahead of other boys in grade level, proficiency, or interests, or he may be an inmate likely to be in school for a longer period of time. The mechanics of tutoring vary with the teacher and the subject matter. In some instances, the teacher assigns reading material he thinks will interest a particular student who reads the material by himself and later discusses it with the teacher.

Teachers feel that the constraints of the larger system make a conventional approach—course outline and textbooks—impractical. If he started at the beginning of a textbook and attempted to cover it chapter by chapter, a teacher might have a complete turnover of students by the time a few chapters were covered. Short-range, frequently repeated lesson plans are more practical.

A similar situation exists in the shop section of the school. Even though sentenced inmates are usually held longer than the nonsentenced, their length of stay also seems too short for conventional goals.

> This is not a vocational training program—not like in a regular trade school. . . . Vocational training takes time . . . how can you expect to suddenly teach a kid a trade when he has never had any

experience at all with these things? So the boys do learn some things; but we don't claim to be making carpenters out of them. Really, the most important thing we try to do is to get them to think. We try to point out that the things which they have done are wrong—that they can't get along in the future if they continue to be socially maladjusted.

EFFECTS OF ENVIRONMENT

Educationally, jail school students are a diverse lot. Considering their age (seventeen to twenty) we expect most inmates to be in eleventh or twelfth grade, if not graduated from high school. Instead, a few boys have dropped out before entering high school, many left as soon as it was legal, and an occasional boy has attended college. Students vary greatly in ability, but as one teacher said: "Most of them are just too far gone. They're too far behind in their schooling, and they just don't care."

Since they do not test students or make use of public school records, teachers devise their own ways to determine students' deficiencies and interests.

I . . . have a little test which I give them sometimes—just something I made up myself. It just has some basic addition, subtraction, multiplication, and so forth on it. . . . If he says he's interested in physics, then I sit down and talk to him about physics for a few minutes. . . . But we get them with all abilities. So you have to find out what they can do and what they are interested in.

Another sort of problem arises for teachers when students behind the others do not want them to know it. Rather than be embarrassed, they want the same work as other inmates, even though it is too advanced for them. Teachers cope with this problem by first giving the student the same assignment and gradually assigning him less difficult material.

The high rate of turnover in the school also makes grading students impractical. Teachers check daily assignments for accuracy and mark them "fair," "good," or "excellent," but:

No, usually we don't [give grades]. The inmates aren't here long enough. ... The only time we give grades ... is when an inmate is still registered in another school and is continuing his education here.

If the jail sends the school legally and educationally heterogeneous recruits, they are relatively homogeneous in social background. While most inmates come from lower socioeconomic areas of the city and county, they differ in two ways—race and gang membership. Over the years, there has been an apparent change in the racial composition of the jail. The trend is toward an increasing proportion of Negro inmates, and people of Puerto Rican and Mexican descent may have increased. School personnel link the changes to new kinds of inmate behavior:

[Administrator to staff member:] I think there's a lot more of just sheer brutality now than there used to be. [Staff member:] You know, Frank [administrator], what you were saying about the fights. I can remember when they used to body punch each other. Two guys'd get up there [on the tier]—stand about so far apart—they'd wrap some cloth around their hands. ... [Frank:] Yeah, but it wasn't the kind of brutality that you find up on the tiers these days. Back when they had kangaroo courts they might strongarm a guy and take all his money away, but after they got his money, they left him alone. There was none of this stuff with four or five guys getting him in a back cell and beating his head off.

Thus, its environment—this time the larger community—affects the school by changing its racial composition. We may attribute the change in inmate composition to similar changes in the larger community, to differential law enforcement, or still other factors. We don't know how accurate teachers' perceptions of changes in inmate behavior are. Nevertheless, the perceived change in inmate behavior has indirect, yet important, consequences for the school. Some teachers feel black students "close them out." When there is violence on the tiers (conflict between blacks and whites, between warring gangs, competing cliques, or individuals) jail personnel punish all inmates by denying them such privileges as going to school. When inmates are emotionally upset by what happens on the tiers, behavior in school may be affected. It is the response of both inmates and jail personnel to violence, not the actual violence, that most affects the school.

The school's lack of control over the number of recruits it gets also has important consequences for its operation. Police and courts control the supply of inmates. According to the number of young men detained or released from jail, there are daily fluctuations in class size in the academic section. A teacher may have fourteen students one day, only four the next. What happens in the vocational section depends on the courts. Judges may sentence young misdemeanants to the county jail, the city jail, the prison farm for youth, or the state youth authority. Changes in sentencing procedures result in many young offenders being sent to institutions other than the county jail.

> [Administrator to observer:] Undoubtedly you've heard about what's been happening. They took away my sentenced boys. So I didn't have anybody in the shops. Not enough to keep them open. [Observer:] Is this just temporary? [Administrator:] Who knows? They just started transferring them over to the city jail. And they took them all. . . . Didn't even tell me. If we don't get them back, my boss will have to act.

Decisions made by nonschool officials can threaten an entire program.

CONCLUSION

In this analysis of a county jail school, we have seen some of the effects of control of recruits by an organization outside but closely allied to the school. School personnel face a high rate of turnover in the student population, uncertainty about how long a student will stay, changes in the racial composition of the students, and such fluctuation in their numbers that entire programs sometimes come to a stop. The staff responds by eliminating such common educational practices as checking previous school records, classification by academic achievement, course outlines, formal testing, and grades. Instead, they put students in the classes they will least disrupt, use short-range, frequently repeated lesson plans, show many movies, uncover deficiencies and interests by talking with students, and work with them individually. In one teacher's words, "We just try to help them as best we can."

Although it is an extreme case, the jail's school is not unique. Both the community at large and specific groups and organizations shape the school's goals and daily practice, probably most successfully through control over students (Clark, 1960). Sometimes such control is as dramatic in effect as federal efforts to integrate schools. It may be as accepted as the expectations of many parents that their children's vacation will coincide with Christian holidays. The most general point is a simple one. Through their ties to outside groups, students may change schools as much as or more than schools change them.

NOTE

1. This is the average length of stay of the 489 non-sentenced inmate students who were released between September 30, 1967, and February 15, 1968. When the 25 students who had been in the jail school longest are excluded, the average drops to 14.5 days. About one half of the inmates were detained for fewer than 11 days; the mode is 7 days. The non-sentenced inmate's length of stay depends on factors beyond the control of school personnel: whether the inmate has a lawyer or must wait to be assigned a public defender, the amount of bond and whether someone posts bond for him, the number of cases on the court dockets, and the speed with which the case is tried once a trial date has been set.

Because most sentenced school inmates were transferred from the county jail to the city jail during the period on which the preceding computations are based, I did not compute the average length of stay for sentenced inmates. School personnel estimate the present average sentence to be about 3 months.

REFERENCES

CLARK, B. R. (1960) The Open Door College. New York: McGraw-Hill.

GROSS, N. (1965) "The sociology of education," pp. 128-152 in R. K. Merton et al. (eds.) Sociology Today. New York: Harper Torchbooks.

MENNERICK, L. A. (1971) "The impact of the external environment on a county jail school." Ph.D. dissertation. Northwestern University.

OLSEN, M. G. (1968) The Process of Social Organization. New York: Holt, Rinehart & Winston.

ZALD, M. N. (1960) "The correctional institution for juvenile offenders: an analysis of organizational 'character.' " Social Problems 8 (Summer): 57-67.

A School Is a Lousy Place To Learn Anything in

HOWARD S. BECKER
Department of Sociology
Northwestern University

Institutions create myths to explain to their participants and the public generally what they do, how they do it, why society needs it done, and how successful they are. Every institution fails in some measure to do the job it promises, and its functionaries find it necessary to explain both that they are trying to do better and that the disparity between promise and performance does not exist, is not serious, or occurs only rarely. Institutional apologias divert our attention from the way the very organization of an institution produces its failures. Further, they divert us from comparisons which might show how others, under a different name and rhetoric, actually perform the institution's characteristic function more effectively.

Schools tell us that people learn in them something they would not otherwise know. Teachers, who know that something, teach it to their pupils. Schools are said to pass the cultural heritage of our society to succeeding generations, both generally in elementary and high school and more differentiatedly in colleges and graduate and professional schools.

Finally, while educators readily admit the shortcomings of schools, they do not conceive that anything in the essence of a school might produce those shortcomings or that any other institutional form might do the job better.

Though the evidence is both too vast to master and too scanty to allow firm conclusions when the great number and variety of schools is taken into account, it suggests that schools do not achieve the results they set out to achieve. Students do not learn what the school proposes to teach them. Colleges do not make students more liberal and humane (Jacob, 1957: 5), nor do they have any great effect on students' intellectual development and learning (Astin, 1968). Medical school training has little effect on the quality of medicine a doctor practices (Petersen, et al., 1956; Clute, 1963). Actors considered expert by their peers have seldom gone to drama school (Hoffman, n.d.). The spectacle of elementary and secondary education gives credence to Herndon's (1968: 79) wry hypothesis that nobody learns anything in school, but middle-class children learn enough elsewhere to make it appear that schooling is effective; since lower-class children don't learn the material elsewhere, the schools' failure to teach them is apparent.

This brief and selective review of the evidence suggests that educational mythology presents an unrealistic picture of the efficacy of schooling. If schools are ineffective, we can consider how their organization might contribute to that ineffectiveness. Our studies of trade schools and apprenticeships allow us to compare the two and see how the organization of each interferes with doing the job it sets out to do.

The following characterization of how schools work grows out of the continuing comparisons generated by our study of trade schools and on-the-job training situations. The various studies have highlighted one or another dimension of educational organization which I have then applied to conventional schools as well. The comparison suggests structural reasons for the schools' educational failures. By constructing an ideal type, a model of a school at its most school-like, we can understand the dynamics of more mixed cases.

COMPLEX SUBJECT MATTER

We set up a school to teach arithmetic or reading, barbering or beauty culture, when we think the subject matter too complex and difficult to be learned in haphazard ordinary life. The student, we say, must master certain "basic" conceptions before he can understand the more complicated structures erected on that base; otherwise he will flounder unnecessarily and never really understand the little he learns. Further, he will suffer a confusion that may be emotionally upsetting, even traumatic, and thus compound the difficulties of learning.

The complexity may lie in the subject matter itself. We think it foolish for a person who cannot read to start by attempting written material of the variety and difficulty one might run into in the ordinary world. We give him simplified materials—short words, simple sentences, a small vocabulary. We teach mathematics by starting with simple concepts of number and relation; we think it easier for children to learn "addition facts" than more abstract conceptions.

The complexity may lie in the social situation the student will later use his knowledge in rather than in the material itself. Techniques of barbering may not be complicated, but we believe a student may have difficulty learning them if he must simultaneously take into account the possible reactions of customers whose hair he has butchered in a beginner-like way. So we set up our school in a way that minimizes the student's anxiety. Barber colleges recruit customers by providing cheap haircuts. Anyone who pays $.75 for a haircut forfeits his right to complain; if he wants a $3.00 haircut, he knows where he can get it, and so does the student barber, who masters his anxiety over complaints by writing his customers off as skid row winos or cheapskates. Similarly, teachers in the barber school Woods (this issue) studied made it their business to tidy up particularly bad jobs done by students. (Medical schools use similar mechanisms.)

CURRICULUM

In principle, a curriculum could be tailor-made for each

student; the complexities of the subject could be simplified to achieve the uniquely best way for him to learn. In practice, schools develop standardized curricula. They arrange the material in some order of increasing complexity, an order usually thought of as the "natural" or "normal" way to approach the subject. They decide what minimum amount of knowledge will be acceptable. They decide on a schedule, time periods in which the student is to learn particular batches of material. They produce, in short, a curriculum, which rests on a conception, usually uninspected, of a normal student who can do that much work and grasp that much material in the time allotted. The eleven-week quarter and the fifteen-week semester are common examples. Anyone who could learn the material more efficiently if it were presented in a different order will have difficulty, as will anyone who needs more or less time than allotted.

Schools could teach students individually, and occasionally make provision to do so. More typically, they process students in batches, treating them as if each were the prototypical normal student for whom they constructed the curriculum. Being part of such a batch naturally constrains the student to behave, as best he can, as though he were prototypical; it is the easiest way to fit into the collective activity he is part of.

TEACHERS

The curriculum necessarily differs substantially from what competent practitioners of the skill or art in question know how to do, for they do not divide what they know into more and less basic components and seldom see any particular order in which what they know should be presented to a learner. Furthermore, competent practitioners in a subject matter area know only by accident, if at all, the skills of teaching. The inability of competent practitioners to teach planned curricula arises equally with such general topics as arithmetic or reading and with specialized skills like cutting and setting hair or driving an automobile. I may be a proficient user of mathematics and a skilled driver and unable to teach a child either one. Ordinary practitioners in a particular subject, finally, have other things to do than teach beginners, and are ordinarily not available for instructional tasks.

So schools require teachers whose principal work is to teach the planned curriculum to batches of normal students. While teachers want to do their work in the easiest, least troublesome way, they also wish to demonstrate to themselves and others that their work produces results. Do a teacher's pupils know something, when he finishes the standard curriculum, that they did not know before, something worth knowing, something attributable to his efforts? Is it a true grasp of the material such that the student can use it in everyday life? Can he read well enough to get about in a literacy-demanding society? Does he know the craft skills (of welding, nursing, hair-cutting, teaching, writing, or whatever) well enough to work adequately with professional peers? Has he mastered the liberal arts well enough to use the knowledge and sensibility they provide to enrich his private life and inform his public activities?

Teachers assume that the student is as inferior in knowledge as he usually is in age (Geer, 1968). They assume that what they know, the student needs to know. They may want to take his opinions into account, but they do not propose to let him decide which portions of the curriculum he will learn. They insist on having the upper hand in the relationship, searching for ways to augment and solidify control when it is disputed.

Because the teacher devotes his full-time effort to teaching, his own knowledge of what actual situations require may be faulty. This is especially obvious in trade schools, where the trade may change substantially after the teacher leaves it, but it occurs in varying degrees in more academic schools as well. Uncertainty about the teacher's knowledge aggravates problems of control and deepens everyone's sense that school training may not be adequate and may require some checking.

PUPILS

Teachers necessarily have pupils. The relationship might be interesting if pupils had more power over its dimensions and content, but the major say on those matters, by common consent of both parties, belongs to the teacher. Students typically (though not always) concede that the teacher knows more about the subject they want to learn than they do; if he did not, there would be little point in studying with him. (Students may refuse to concede the teacher's superiority when they attend school, as they often do, for some purpose other than learning: to avoid being charged as a truant, to secure a draft exemption, or to meet a legal requirement for some other desired activity.) They want to learn and expect that the teacher will help them, even though his activities seem to have no immediate or discernible relation to that goal. When they lose faith in his authority, they refuse to accept the standard curriculum, and the teacher's job becomes more difficult; he must persuade or coerce students into doing what he thinks best.

Students want to know whether they have learned something as they proceed through the curriculum. Their desire may reflect an uncertainty of the curriculum itself, but more likely reflects a concern with their own abilities. They think a normal student should be able to learn what the curriculum proposes in the time allotted. Are they normal? Have they learned what they should? Do they just think they learned it, while in truth they missed the point or are doing it the wrong way?

They ask themselves these questions because the school often fails to tell them whether their understanding is correct, their skill adequate. They need the answers to see whether their allocation of time and effort needs change and to confront deeper questions about the suitability of what they have attempted. Is this the right course for me? The right school? Do I want to spend any more of my life in pursuits like this? These questions arise for graduate students, students in professional schools, and students in trade schools equally, though trade school students have made a lesser commitment and can more easily take remedial action if they decide they have made a mistake.

TESTS AND EVALUATIONS

The setting in which teachers teach and students learn will be quite different, of necessity and by design, from the world in which students use what they have learned. The materials taught differ from the fully complex materials the world contains. When the student completes the work the school lays out for him, neither he nor his teacher can be sure there are not crucial differences between what he has been taught and what will later be required of him. So teachers—who want to know how their students will fare when they leave school—students— who wonder whether they are truly prepared for the tasks they will now have to do—and the rest of the world—which wonders what it can expect of the graduates—combine their desires for a working knowledge of what is being accomplished in a demand for tests and other evaluative procedures. A formal program of evaluation tells teachers they are doing their job competently, students that they have learned what they came for, and employers, parents, legislators, and others that the school is doing what is expected of it.

The chief problem in testing students and evaluating their performance is to concoct tests isomorphic to the real world situations in which the student will exercise his skills. How do we test whether a student can successfully cut the hair of a fussy, middle-class executive who worries about his looks, when the only material available for him to demonstrate his skill on is a sixty-year-old drunk who falls asleep in the chair and whom both student and instructor know cannot and will not complain? Beauty colleges solve this problem (as does the state barber board in conducting licensing examinations) by requiring the examinee to provide his own subject (usually a relative or friend); medical schools do not let students perform important or dangerous procedures without supervision by more experienced, licensed physicians. Neither solution is fully effective, since each avoids some of the most cogent difficulties in social relationships. But both represent a high in isomorphism between school and practice compared to the written examinations and problem-solving exercises graduate schools, to take a notorious example, habitually use. These more typical examinations differ in gross ways from the tasks examinees will later be called on to do. It is commonplace, but true, to suggest that such tests mainly measure the ability to take tests.

We seldom argue that conventional tests measure the actual skills students are supposed to have learned. Rather, we believe that the test, while not a direct measure, is nevertheless highly correlated with the ability to exercise those skills, though the mechanism by which the alleged correlation occurs is seldom investigated or demonstrated. Common observation suggests the belief is unfounded; we seldom find hard evidence of such correlations. Instead, we rely on test results for want of anything better. In any event, the skills required to perform well on school examinations may not be the same skills required to perform adequately in the situations the school trains people for.

Another difficulty in addition to the divergence between test and real life, is that tests are usually taken at the convenience of the tester, at a time set by the periodicity of the normal curriculum, at the end of the quarter, semester, or year, when the designated material has been covered. The test thus does not measure a student's ultimate knowledge, but his knowledge as of the time of the examination. This feature, among others, increases the student's anxiety, so that the conventional test in some part measures not knowledge, but the student's ability to withstand or cope with anxiety (Mechanic, 1962).

SCHOOL REWARDS AND STUDENT CULTURE

Schools seldom use evaluations of students' performances in an advisory way, to help the student discover areas of weakness which can be strengthened by a changed allocation of effort. Instead, they incorporate the results of such evaluations—grades will do as the generic term—into permanent records, on whose basis people and institutions make decisions bearing on students' futures. Schools vary in the degree to which they allow examination results to become fateful beyond their immediate academic relevance. If grades have fateful consequences, students find it necessary to orient their efforts toward getting good ones; if tests are not isomorphic to the situations in which the abilities being tested will be used, students will have to divert time and effort from what the school wants to teach to what is needed for a good grade. This untoward consequence occurs only when tests do not measure and require the knowledge the school wishes to teach. When the two are the same, the school's reward system evokes exactly the learning teachers desire.

We found an extreme example of the constraint grading and evaluation exercised on students' allocations of their efforts in our study of a college (Becker et al., 1968). Students' grade point averages, being the chief measure available and presumably reasonably accurate, fair, and comparable, affected most other rewards a student might want (or not want to be denied) during and after college. For example, college rules specified a minimum grade point average for initiation into a fraternity or sorority, for holding major office in campus organizations, and for staying in school and graduating. Grades also affected a student's chances of getting into professional or graduate school, as well as the kind of job he might get on graduation. Grades even affected his social life: he might find it harder to meet eligible girls if he did not belong to a fraternity or could not participate in extracurricular activities because of low grades; girls were often reluctant to get involved with anyone who might flunk out. Since whatever a student wanted had to be paid for in high grades, few students felt they could safely avoid learning what was needed for tests. It is hard to say what the desired outcomes of a college's educational efforts are. But if they are a change in values and the acquisition of certain intellectual skills, students might be diverted from such goals by the necessity of studying for exams not requiring those abilities.

When what tests require differs from what the school wants to teach, and when the school rewards good test performance heavily, the structure of the school will systematically divert student effort. In this sense, and to the degree that these conditions are met, schools are structurally self-defeating. Where students have the opportunity to interact and develop collective conceptions of their situation and how it ought to be handled, they may develop a student culture which amplifies and extends this effect. When students agree they must do certain things to give a good performance for evaluation, and when that information is passed on to new students, each student need not experience the disparity and the constraint himself. He knows beforehand, in the way any functioning culture allows us to know, what is coming and how to deal with it. A student culture which advises grade-getting as an optimal strategy decreases the likelihood that students will attempt other strategies, though it does not make that impossible.

Since some students do learn some things that schools want to teach, the above analysis deals with the extreme case. Where some of the conditions outlined above do not obtain, schools will be more successful than the analysis suggests.

ON-THE-JOB TRAINING

The chief alternative to learning things in school is to learn them on the job, especially if we define on-the-job training broadly. So defined, it includes not only the conventional apprenticeship in a trade, but all the casual learning that goes on in the course of everyday living, the kind of learning Goodman (1968) and Holt (1967) have called to our attention as the way children learn to talk and most other things. Think of living your daily life as a job to give the notion its full meaning. Though I speak mainly of occupational training, keep the larger relevances in mind.

The apprentice learns on the job, in the place where people do in a routine way whatever members of his trade do. He finds himself surrounded from the outset by the characteristic sights, sounds, situations, activities, and problems he will face as long as he remains in the trade (if we reasonably assume the trade does not change in the short run). The butcher's apprentice

(Marshall, this issue) works in a meat market, where journeymen break down carcasses, cut them into conventionally defined pieces of meat, trim them, price them, and package them. The apprentice ironworker (Haas, this issue) works on a building under construction, where journeymen place beams and girders, rivet and weld them together, place rods for reinforced concrete, do finishing work, and take dangerous walks on narrow beams in high places. (Similarly, the small child, learning to talk, lives in a world in which most of the kinds of talk that go on, simple and complex, go on around him in person, on the radio, or on television; Goodman, 1968). Thus, the learner sees the kind of work he is to learn in all its tangled complexity from the first day, instead of being introduced to those complexities a step at a time in a carefully constructed curriculum. He suffers whatever traumas may arise from realizing all there is to learn. Some apprentices give up their ambitions quickly when they realize what they have gotten into, but those who remain have a pretty good idea of what they are in for from the start. They see the technical difficulties, the dangers, the social complications that may arise with employers and customers, and even the informal requirements of making it with one's work peers.

One consequence follows the immediate accessibility of the full round of activities characteristic of an apprentice's trade. He can participate in these activities right away or on any idiosyncratic schedule he can work out with his fellow workers. No one can learn everything at once, but no principle or rule prevents the apprentice from learning a little of this today, a little of that tomorrow, things in some order no one ever thought of before, or learning to the point where he wants to stop and then switching to something else. He need not, when he wants to learn a certain procedure, wait until its time in a prearranged schedule; nor need he learn something he is not ready for, thinks uninteresting, frightening, or unncessary. The learner makes his own curriculum.

TEACHERS

This curriculum is created with the aid of people who know

more than he does, who must be persuaded to assist him, or at least not to interfere with his own efforts. Because the learning situation is the real work world—an actual meat market or construction site—no one functions as an official teacher. Everyone has his own job to do, his own set of occupational constraints and rewards. The apprentice does not have a teacher's time and attention guaranteed to him as does a pupil in a conventional school.

This leaves the actual training to the apprentice's own initiative. Competent practitioners will teach him if he can persuade them to, and actual training is thus in some part a function of such formally extraneous traits as the degree of his aggressiveness. A pushy punk learns more than a quiet young man. An ideology common among journeymen suggests that if an apprentice is any good, he will make you teach him; if he does not push, he probably does not have what it takes. This differs diametrically from a conventional school in which learning occurs at the teacher's initiative: you move on when the teacher thinks you are ready.

In such a system, no one rests his self-esteem, reputation, or claim to having done a decent day's work on the amount his students learn. While everyone cares in general that the apprentices eventually learn their trade, no particular person can be blamed or has it on his conscience if any particular apprentice or group of apprentices fails to learn. Teaching is no one's job in particular, so it is no one's fault if no learning occurs.

Two consequences follow from the failure to assign teaching responsibility. On the one hand, when teaching does occur, it is not overlaid with the teacher's own worries about how he is doing; teacher and apprentice can concentrate on the learner's difficulties. Where the teacher has no responsibility, he cannot misuse or fail to meet it. On the other hand, an apprentice may not be taught anything, since he may not be aggressive enough to force anyone to teach him.

EXTERNAL CONSTRAINTS

The characteristic virtues of each kind of learning situation breed characteristic difficulties and vices. Schools divorce themselves from the problems of the everyday world in an effort to make learning easier. They thus create a need for evaluative mechanisms and thus divert student effort from learning to efforts to be evaluated more highly. On-the-job training, in and of the everyday world, provides a realistic and individualized learning setting. But it does that at the cost of making teaching and learning vulnerable to potent external constraints.

The chief constraint arises from setting the educational encounter in a real-life enterprise which has its own problems and imperatives. Meat markets have, as their main purpose, to sell meat profitably to customers. Ironworkers work for a company whose main business is to construct a building or a bridge. Interns (who also undergo a kind of on-the-job training) work in hospitals whose main business is to treat illness (Miller, 1970). Each enterprise requires potential learners and teachers alike to contribute what they can to the success of the enterprise as the price of continued participation.

But the required contribution may prevent teaching or learning. Potential teachers may not have time for it, because of the press of more important business. When journeymen butchers prepare for a steak sale, they do not have time to teach apprentices. When senior physicians handle medical emergencies, they have no time to teach interns. Opportunities for on-the-job learning vary inversely with the amount of work the enterprise must turn out.

Similarly, the apprentice's labor and time may be used for necessary work for the total enterprise that no one else wants to do. An apprentice ironworker's first jobs are fire watch (looking for possible fires set by sparks from welding and riveting operations) and getting coffee for the journeymen. These jobs are not entirely uneducational—going for coffee prepares the novice to "run the iron"—but apprentices do them not for that reason but because people want them done and the apprentice, lowest man on the totem pole, gets the honor. Apprentice meatcutters start out running the wrapping machine, which packages, seals, and labels the meat. The wrapping machine requires no skill, and working on it falls to the one who cannot do anything else; the work may familiarize the novice with the various cuts of meat, but is not a big step in becoming a butcher. An apprentice may run the wrapping machine for the three years in a large meat department solely because the other workmen, knowing more, can be profitably used elsewhere. Marshall saw one apprentice work on the wrapping machine for three months until a new apprentice was hired; then apprentice 1 was taught new skills while apprentice 2 ran the wrapping machine. No further new apprentice was hired, and apprentice 2 continued to run the wrapping machine. Someone had to. The first apprentice received superior training by the accident of being hired three months earlier and thus being advantageously placed with respect to the needs of the total enterprise.

Another external constraint limiting the opportunity to learn lies in the potential cost—to fellow workers, employers, customers, or the public—of allowing an unskilled apprentice to undertake some task. Because teaching hospitals may be held liable for the damage done a patient, they limit what medical students can do to patients in furthering their own learning. Ironworkers do not allow apprentices to do things that might jeopardize the safety of fellow workers. Meat cutters give apprentices more practice cutting up meat in markets that serve poor populations. The cost of mistakes made on cheap cuts of pork can more easily be absorbed than mistakes made on the expensive steaks sold in markets in more well-to-do neighborhoods.

Some of the things a novice ought to learn (or would like to learn) may occur infrequently during his period of training. A school would make some provision to cover this material, so that the student's competence would not depend on the accidents of history. Medical schools compromise, necessarily, on this point; they systematically *teach* about various diseases, but whether a student has clinical experience with those diseases is left to the chance of whether a patient with a certain disease appears during the student's tenure.

Gross effects of the external environment on the learning

situation result from changes in the economy. A depression (or the memory of one, in some trades) may cause journeymen to fear the competition of too many qualified workmen. In consequence, they systematically withhold training and keep apprentices at the classic apprenticeship tasks of sweeping the shop and running out for coffee. Boom times make it harder to get prospective trainees; with more work to be done, apprentices must quickly be pushed into more responsible positions; if they feel ill-used, they may quit, and the enterprise needs their labor to meet its commitments. Under these circumstances, a trainee may be taught thoroughly and rapidly.

In short, what one can learn on the job and who will teach it depend on contingencies unrelated to education or training. The learning situation exists to do some quite different job and is subject to the constraints emanating from the external world, any of which may interfere directly in the novice's training. Many of these interferences have nothing whatever to do with any attribute of the novice, neither his skill or aptitude, nor his aggressiveness and initiative. The defect is structural.

EVALUATION

Even if people who learn on the job never take formal examinations, they do not escape evaluation, which occurs continuously as they go about their daily business. Everything they do is what people in that line of work do, and everyone in a position to observe their performance can immediately see whether they have done it satisfactorily. No person with special training need be present to make the evaluation; most people on the scene can do it. The evaluators not only know the work the novice attempts, but are the very people the novice must please to be successful. On-the-job training thus avoids completely any disparity between what the school tests and what the real world requires. Because the evaluators are part of that real world and what they require is the test, the two are the same.

Placing the process of evaluation in the midst of the work setting has interesting consequences:

(1) The learner can take his tests any time he feels ready. Every novice will want to test himself or allow himself to be tested to convince both others and himself that he has mastered some important skill. In schools, tests can be taken only at stated intervals, when the tester gives them; often the student must take them at the time they are given or suffer a serious penalty. Since the on-the-job trainee's test will consist of doing something that could be done every day (or almost every day, allowing for weekly or seasonal variations in workloads), he can take it at his discretion, simply by announcing that he thinks he can do a particular task. Someone will give him the chance, and both novice and observer can see the result. The test is self-scoring and self-interpreting, since the product either does or does not pass muster in the same way the world usually evaluates it.

(2) Because the test consists of performing some routine task, an apprentice can take it repeatedly, without having to wait for any special time, until he finally performs successfully. Unlike the typical school, in which scores are averaged over some time period, only the last test counts. Since the test can be repeated, and since the learner takes the test when he feels ready, he feels less anxiety than over a conventional school test. The results are less fateful.

(3) Because his progress is immediately observable, the learner can make a good or bad reputation among the people he will be working with once he has become a full-fledged member of the group. The possibility can cause considerable anxiety. School typically shelters the student from having his bad mistakes known to the people he will eventually join, but mistakes made on the job are fully seen by those people. Further, while school does not let really serious mistakes occur (because it simplifies the curriculum in ways making that impossible), learning on the job allows costly, even fatal, mistakes to occur, because the actual work cannot be successfully sealed off. An apprentice meatcutter can ruin an expensive side of beef; an apprentice ironworker can unintentionally cripple or kill another worker. In each case, that reputation may dog the perpetrator for years, especially if he harms a valued colleague (Forsyth and Kolenda, 1966: 132).

(4) Testing on the job is not restricted to technical material. It includes all the relevant human relations skills as well. Haas provides a detailed example in his analysis of "binging." Ironworkers must

demonstrate their ability to participate adequately in this earthy teasing before those already established accept them as trustworthy. Schools do not test these skills; on-the-job situations invariably do.

(5) Because the testing occurs so much at the insistence of the novice, and because he may not wish to be tested in all or even in very many areas, a person who learns on the job may never be tested on a great variety of matters. Insofar as testing has value for either the learner or those who have to work with him or use his services, that value may well be lost. (This is another way of saying that the apprentice may not be taught more than a few of the trade's characteristic skills.)

RELATIONS TO THE WORLD OF WORK

Educators, as I have already suggested, construct a standard curriculum which includes what they regard as the essential elements anyone must learn to be certified as knowing particular subjects, or as fit to occupy a particular social or occupational position. As we have seen, learning on the job in no way assures that any student will learn such a common core of knowledge. In this, learning on the job realistically reflects the character of most jobs and occupations.

Hughes (1951) has suggested that any job or occupation, any named kind of work, actually consists of a bundle of tasks. Some of those tasks may be taken to be symbolic of the whole, as when we think of courtroom pleading as the definitive legal task. Ordinarily, no single member of the occupation does the full range of tasks associated with it. Differentiation and specialization characterize most kinds of work, so that a member of the occupation may actually do only one or two tasks from the bundle. A school requires students to learn the entire bundle, in case they are called on to perform any of them, but on-the-job training allows a student to learn, at a minimum, only one, while still becoming a full-fledged member of the trade. On-the-job training thus reflects realistically the demands of the labor market, operating on the assumption that, if a person can get a job doing one of the tasks in the bundle, he knows enough to be an acceptable member of the trade.

Ironworkers present an interesting example of this phenomenon. The characteristic and symbolic act that marks the "real ironworker" is "running the iron," working high above the ground while standing on a four-to-eight inch steel beam. Running the iron takes more nerve than some recruits have, but their failure either to take that test or, if they try, to pass it, does not mean that they cannot be ironworkers. They can do one of the other jobs, requiring more brawn than nerve, such as placing rods for reinforced concrete construction. They will not get the considerable glory that goes with doing the tasks that require bravery, but they can still be ironworkers.

The work world, in short, accommodates what people can do. Apprenticeship and job training prepare people for such a world. They avoid a recruit's difficulties with some portion of the standard curriculum, at the cost of producing a member of the trade who knows less than the complete body of knowledge that might be expected of him.

CONCLUSIONS

I have been discussing ideal types. Real-life educational situations usually contain some mixture of school and on-the-job styles of teaching and learning. Thus, medical schools, beauty schools, and barber colleges are schools, but with strong on-the-job emphases. On the other hand, meatcutters and ironworkers may take classes in some subjects. Ordinarily, when we are anxious to teach people something, we remove teaching from the job and organize a school. The above analysis has as its chief implication that schools are lousy places to learn, precisely because we establish them without considering the circumstances under which other ways of proceeding, perhaps less organized, might be more efficient, more humane, or both. Another equally important implication is that on-the-job training is often no better, for the same reason. The analysis has in general been pessimistic, making it appear impossible for anyone to learn anything. Since people do learn, the analysis is clearly insufficient, and I would like to end by considering how this learning occurs.

I do not suggest that students learn *nothing* in school, only that they typically learn what the school does not intend to teach and do much less well with what the school focuses on. We found an excellent example of this in our study of college students. Students learned effective methods of operating politically on campus. But in academic subjects they devoted themselves to getting good grades, a time-consuming activity that presumably accounts for the lack of attitude change Jacob reports and the lack of effect on academic achievement Astin uncovered. The explanation is that they learned their politics on the job, by acting in the political arena of the campus. Imagine what would happen if someone gave a course in "Operating on Campus," complete with texts, tests, and grades. Students, busy learning how to pass the tests, would never become the effective politicians campus political life produces.

People learn, in spite of the obstacles our analysis suggests, because the schools and job situations in which they learn seldom approach the extreme conditions of these ideal analytic types. Schools are effective, when and where they are, because tests sometimes require what teachers want students to learn, because teachers do not always connect a multitude of other rewards to academic performance, because students are some-times incapable of developing a culture which maintains and spreads counterfaculty perspectives. On-the-job training is often effective because someone does have time to do a little teaching, because the enterprise allows enough leeway for the apprentice to make some mistakes without costing others too much, because the things that can interfere with his learning are fortuitous occurrences rather than structural necessities.

On-the-job training, then, for all the difficulties I have mentioned, is more likely to produce educational successes. Nevertheless, I do not propose that we immediately convert all education to an apprenticeship model. Substantial difficulties are associated with that model. Students may be denied the teaching they want, due to the exigencies and constraints of the real-life situation in which the training occurs. Students may learn very little of what we would like to see them know, even though they will probably learn a little something.

Nor is it easy to set up apprenticelike training situations. It requires the specification of educational goals in a more exact way than is common in schools. When schools state "educational objectives," they generally content themselves with pious generalities. If you want to create an on-the-job training situation, you must go much farther and find a place in the everyday world where people ordinarily act just as you wish your trainees to act, where the very skills, attitudes, and sensibilities you wish to inculcate are embodied in the daily activities of people trainees will be allowed to associate with. It is often difficult to find a place which wishes to be used as a site for an educational enterprise.

In addition, we sometimes cannot specify our objectives clearly. We may believe that we are training people for an unknown future. We do not know what we want them to know, because we cannot specify the problems and situations they will have to cope with. This may be because the situations that lie ahead of them are too complicated for us to deal with in detail or because we believe the world is going to change so much that we cannot forecast how things will be and thus what a person will need to know to act effectively. Given such a diagnosis, we generally settle for inculcating proper orientations from which students will be able to deduce correct lines of action in specific cirumstances, general skills which can be used in a variety of situations, and an ability to learn new material as it becomes available.

We will always have schools, because we will often find ourselves in the dilemma of preparing people for unknown futures. A minimum use of the present analysis might then be to broaden educators' perspectives so that they will be aware of the possibilities of apprenticelike training that may be available to them (Beck and Becker, 1969) and not engage unnecessarily in activities that actively defeat the very ends they seek. Such irrationality can only perpetuate the troubles our schools are already in and deepen the mistrust so many people have of them.

REFERENCES

ASTIN, A. W. (1968) "Undergraduate achievement and institutional 'excellence.'" Science 161 (August 16): 661-668.

BECK, B. and H. S. BECKER (1969) "Modest proposals for graduate programs in sociology." Amer. Sociologist 4 (August): 227-234.

BECKER, H. S., B. GEER, and E. C. HUGHES (1968) Making the Grade: The Academic Side of College Life. New York: John Wiley.

CLUTE, K. F. (1963) The General Practitioner: A Study of Medical Education and Practice in Ontario and Nova Scotia. Toronto: Univ. of Toronto Press.

FORSYTH, S. and P. M. KOLENDA (1966) "Competition, cooperation and group cohesion in the ballet company." Psychiatry 29 (May): 123-145.

GEER, B. (1968) "Teaching," pp. 560-565 in Volume 15 of the International Encyclopedia of the Social Sciences. New York: Macmillan and Free Press.

GOODMAN, P. (1968) "Mini-schools: a prescription for the reading problem." New York Rev. of Books 9 (January 4): 16-18.

HERNDON, J. (1968) The Way It Spozed To Be. New York: Bantam.

HOFFMAN, T. (n.d.) "The acting student: species, habitat, behavior." (unpublished)

HOLT, J. (1967) How Children Learn. New York: Pitman.

HUGHES, E. C. (1951) "Studying the nurse's work." Amer. J. of Nursing 51 (May): 294-295.

JACOB, P. (1957) Changing Values in College: An Exploratory Study of the Impact of College Teaching. New York: Harper.

MECHANIC, D. (1962) Students Under Stress. New York: Free Press.

MILLER, S. J. (1970) Prescription for Excellence. Chicago: Aldine.

PETERSON, O. L., L. P. ANDREWS, R. S. SPAIN, and B. G. GREENBERG (1956) "An analytical study of North Carolina general practice, 1953-1954." J. of Medical Education 31 (December): 1-165.